Proclamation 4

Aids for Interpreting
the Lessons of the Church Year

Pentecost 3

David G. Buttrick

Series C

FORTRESS PRESS   PHILADELPHIA

Biblical quotations, unless otherwise noted, are the author's translations or are from the Revised Standard Version of the Bible, copyright 1946, 1952, © 1971, 1973 by the Division of Christian Education of the National Council of the Churches of Christ in the U.S.A., and are used by permission.

COPYRIGHT © 1989 BY FORTRESS PRESS

All rights reserved. No part of this publication may be reproduced, stored in a retrieval system, or transmitted in any form or by any means, electronic, mechanical, photocopying, recording, or otherwise, without the prior permission of the publisher, Fortress Press.

Library of Congress Cataloging-in-Publication Data

Proclamation 4 : aids for interpreting the lessons of the church year / Christopher R. Seitz.
    p. cm.
    Consists of 28 volumes in 3 series designated A, B, and C, which correspond to the cycles of the three-year lectionary. Each series contains 8 basic volumes with the following titles:
Advent/Christmas, Epiphany, Lent, Holy Week, Easter, Pentecost 1, Pentecost 2, and Pentecost 3.
    ISBN 0–8006–4160–4
    1. Bible—Liturgical lessons, English. I. Seitz, Christopher R.
BS391.2.S37 1988
264′.34—dc19   88–10982

Printed in the United States of America   1–4160

95   94   93   92   91   2   3   4   5   6   7   8   9   10

Contents

The Twentieth Sunday after Pentecost	5
The Twenty-first Sunday after Pentecost	12
The Twenty-second Sunday after Pentecost	20
The Twenty-third Sunday after Pentecost	26
The Twenty-fourth Sunday after Pentecost	34
The Twenty-fifth Sunday after Pentecost	40
The Twenty-sixth Sunday after Pentecost	47
Christ the King The Last Sunday after Pentecost	54

The Twentieth Sunday after Pentecost

Lutheran	Roman Catholic	Episcopal	Common Lectionary
Hab. 1:1–3; 2:1–4	Hab. 1:2–3; 2:2–4	Hab. 1:1–6 (7–11) 12–13; 2:1–4	Amos 5:6–7, 10–15
2 Tim. 1:3–14	2 Tim. 1:6–8, 13–14	2 Tim. 1:(1–5) 6–14	2 Tim. 1:1–14
Luke 17:1–10	Luke 17:5–10	Luke 17:5–10	Luke 17:5–10

FIRST LESSON: HABAKKUK 1:1–3; 2:1–4

The headlines were bleak around 600 B.C. A Chaldean army was poised at the border about to sweep down on Judah (v. 6). The little land had less than two decades left to live. Internally, the country was in disarray—moral decay, division, and common violence filled the land (v. 3). In such a moment, Habakkuk, a professional temple prophet, composed his careful songs. Like a modern-day poet laureate, Habakkuk was supposed to address occasions. What could he say to Judah?

Habakkuk was more than a mere "professional" because he dared to deal with deep, troubling questions. Like Jeremiah (Jer. 14:9) or some tormented psalmist (Ps. 13:1–2), he launched his questions toward God. "Lord, how long will I cry for help, and you not hear?" (v. 2) If God is good and God is great, then how can catastrophe visit God's people? Why does the world seem to whirl toward destruction if God is in charge? Why? In our world, where ignorant armies still clash by night and public morality is ever sullied by greed, Habakkuk's question is contemporary. How long? indeed!

Like a watchman (Isa. 62:6–7), Habakkuk stares into the future and beyond, into the distant mystery of God's purpose, searching for some answer to his questions. Gradually, an answer seems to form, an answer worth posting in a public place for frantic Judah to see (2:2). The answer is twofold: wait, and be faithful. Wait, because though God's purposes may seem postponed in a broken brutal world, nevertheless God's promises are sure. In time, *God's time* (v. 3), the promise of the kingdom will come. God is faithful and, even in a world askew, is working out divine purpose through all things. Trusting God's promises, we wait.

Our waiting is not a *Waiting for Godot*, however; we do not kill time on an empty stage, chattering in a moral vacuum, waiting for a Godot who will never come. No, we wait in faithfulness.

Verse 4b is a kind of credo: "The righteous shall live by faith." According to the Talmud, the verse is a compendium of all the commandments. So it seemed to the apostle Paul and, of course, to Martin Luther—"The just shall live by faith." Now we must be cautious, and not read Reformation theology back into Habakkuk. Faith for Habakkuk is not mere believing ("Just believe in Jeeeeesus and you'll be saved!"); it is an active, righteous life, faithful to the will of God. The two parts of v. 4 must be kept together; a puffed up person bent toward *numero uno* purposes will fail, but whoever in faith is faithful will live, truly *live* even in the midst of tumbling chaos. According to Habakkuk, God has given us an "upright" way of life to live. Yes, "faith" here does mean to believe the promises of God, a God who is ever faithful. But, "faith" in Habakkuk also must be understood as fidelity, living the obedient life God has called us to live.

Please notice that the passage in Habakkuk should not be narrowed down to the problem of personal suffering. While we human beings do cry out, How long? in moments of personal anguish, Habakkuk's vision is both social and eschatological. He is staring out at a troubled world, violent, unjust, and heedless of God, a world that seems to be rushing headlong toward self-destruction. In such a moment, where is God?

Of course, remember, Habakkuk's question can only be asked by those who believe in a covenant-making God. For an atheist, the chaos of the world is scarcely a theological problem. But for people such as us, who believe that "God is good" and that "God's will will be done," a world awry does pose profound, probing questions. Certainly, we live in a fiercely troubled era in which nuclear threat is terrifyingly real, and in which a hungry half of the human race has an unusually high standard of dying. Is God still working through all things to bring about a good purpose? Or has God simply withdrawn from us, leaving us to our own willful self-destruction? No, Habakkuk affirms the faithfulness of God; what God has promised shall be! We must be faithful too, living before God as God has commanded. "The righteous shall live," sings Habakkuk, "by faithfulness." His word is a good word in our kind of world; a true word of the Lord.

A sermon on the passage might begin with Habakkuk, a thoughtful human being staring into the distance, trying to figure out what's going on in his world. We do, too. So a preacher can raise Habakkuk's profound question with regard to our own world. Will it be difficult to portray both moral chaos and the threat of destruction in the world today? Then a sermon could turn to question God. Where is God in the chaos and, more crucial, what of God's promises? Robert Browning, in a harsh poem, pictures a murderer sitting beside a murdered lover, and adds, "Still God has not said a word." Well, we wonder. Hungry hordes of human beings die daily eating dust in Africa, in Central America terrifying conflict ravages little villages, and in our own land the Pentagon bills for bombs mount up—and God does not say a word! How can we reconcile a world awry with the love of God?

The answer: Patience! If God is patient, working through our sinful freedoms to bring about an eternal purpose for the world, we can stand patiently with God. Look at the cross and see that God can bring resurrection glory out of the depth of human brutality. The risen Christ is a sign that what God wills will be!

Meanwhile, how do we live? We live trusting, indeed clinging, to the promises of God. Think of a wonderful old man eaten away by gangrene, lying in a hospital bed, slapping his one good leg and shouting hoarsely, "Believe the promises!" No matter what the world is like, we are to trust God who in Christ has promised a someday salvation for the world.

But faith is no mere believing against the odds; faith is a life lived. If God's promise is sure, then *now* we can keep faith and live toward the kingdom as good citizens of God in an unGodly world. Faith, true faith, is faithfulness.

Common Lectionary: Amos 5:6–7, 10–15. This is a difficult passage from the Hebrew Bible. The passage from Amos packages a series of separate oracles, a few from the prophet and others from some later source. The oracles are loosely bunched according to a topic: Corruption in the courts. They are rather unusual for Amos because they seem to echo some slight hope of redemption—"Seek the Lord and live"! Let us trace our way through the complicated passage.

Verse 6 (probably not by Amos) picks up words from v. 4b and calls us to "seek the Lord and live" lest we be destroyed by the consuming fire of God's judgment. The image of fire repeats in Amos (see 1:4, 7, 10, 12; 2:2, 5, 12) and is a familiar prophetic formula, perhaps conjuring up a vision of torching by an invading army.

Verse 7 introduces the theme of justice, which, instead of healing broken human relationships, produces nothing but bitterness. Wormwood was a plant with a sharp sour taste and, therefore, a common metaphor for galling circumstances (see Jer. 9:15; 23:15).

Verse 10, "in the gate," refers to a fortified gatehouse built into city walls that offered space for court assemblies—in effect, a courtroom. "They hate him who reproves" refers to a village elder who, in delivering a judicial decision, gets at the truth, separating right from wrong, and, of course, reproving the wrong. "They" are thus accused of showing a total disregard for the judicial system.

Verse 11, another disconnected oracle, points to wealthy urbanites who, through legal chicanery, take over the lands of the poor. Thus, small farmers become sharecroppers who must hand over most of the wheat they grow as a rental fee. The rich in turn are getting richer; they are building lavish stone manor houses and planting lush vineyards. But, says the prophet, pronouncing a futility curse, the rich will never live in their houses or sip their fine wine!

Verse 12 returns to court procedure ("in the gate"), accusing the rich of pressuring the poor and of swaying decisions by bribery.

But vv. 14-15 once more offer a moral alternative, "Seek good, and not evil, that you may live." If the rich will respect true justice, according to God's covenant law, then there is a chance that God "will be gracious to the remnant of Joseph."

The passage is seldom preached; most ministers are not eager to take on the legal profession—or wealthy entrepreneurs for that matter! But, in the Bible, justice is not an abstract ideal. No, God's justice happens in particular places (local courts) and in particular commercial deals (e.g., agribusiness takeovers). There is no doubt that legal recourse in America is exceedingly expensive and, as a result, often beyond the resources of the poor. When access to the courts is easier for the rich than the poor, then God's justice is in jeopardy.

If the passage is preached (and it should emphatically be preached), a preacher might begin by depicting the growing gap in our society between rich and poor, which tends to leave the poor in a position of helplessness. A sermon might then turn to look at the current problem of legal access. The issue is, of course, *theological*; human law is meant to mirror God's own justice. And God, the holy God of Israel, seems to have a special concern for victims. (Did not Jesus Christ end up in court as a condemned prisoner?) So we are called to reform our legal system under the judgment of God. "Seek God and live" is not an invitation to a prayer meeting; it is a call to do true social justice.

SECOND LESSON: 2 TIMOTHY 1:6-14

Whoever wrote 2 Timothy pictures an imprisoned Paul writing words of encouragement to a younger colleague, Timothy, whom he has ordained. The passage has an interesting design. In vv. 6-8, Paul urges Timothy to renew the gift of the Spirit that he has received, to speak the gospel without embarrassment, and to accept suffering bravely. Verses 9-10 appear to be a quoted creed familiar to readers of 2 Timothy. Then, in vv. 11-12, Paul cites himself—he is a preacher who suffers bravely and is not ashamed to speak the gospel. The passage concludes with a final exhortation to faithfulness, which circles back to affirm the gift of the Spirit. Thus vv. 11-14 seem to rehearse the same agenda as vv. 6-8, but in reverse order.

The passage seems to suggest that at ordination ministers receive some special endowment of the Spirit through the laying on of hands (cf. 2 Tim. 1:6; 1 Tim. 4:14), a notion of ministry somewhat more developed than in 1 Corinthians 12.

The creed (or creedal hymn) in vv. 9-10 is of special interest. Possibly it is a two-part confession of faith, designed on a then/now basis. In v. 9, we recall that from the beginning God, the savior, determined to call us to holiness. In v. 10, we realize that God's hidden purpose has been displayed in the epiphany of Jesus Christ, who has dethroned death and brought us life. Probably the phrase "not in virtue of our works but in virtue of [God's] own purpose" is a happy addition to the two-part confession. The two-part theology of the creed—speaking of God's secret purpose for the world and then claiming that God's plan is revealed in the epiphany of Jesus Christ—is typical of later non-Pauline epistles (see, e.g., Eph. 3:1-6).

The passage may seem difficult to preach; it is not. Are we not all ordained by baptism to a common evangelical ministry? Like young Timothy, we should not be ashamed of speaking the gospel whatever opposition (or ridicule) we may encounter (vv. 8, 12). Our speaking is after all part of God's eternal purpose for the human world which has been revealed in Jesus Christ and is on display in the new life he gives (vv. 9-10). So we must stir up the evangelical Spirit that has been poured out on us and, trusting in the risen Christ (v. 12), speak with courage, intelligence, and love (v. 7).

The problem with preaching the passage in most American congregations is that the only suffering we endure is public indifference, and the images of evangelism we have are either unpleasantly religious or the calculated sales techniques of the Church Growth Movement. Of course, the real impetus for evangelism is set forth in the creed that 2 Timothy quotes. All along, God has been working to bring us into a life of free communion, and now, through Christ Jesus, it can be. The true purpose of evangelism is setting folk free for life with God by the liberating word of the gospel.

A sermon on this reading might begin by working off the word "ashamed." When most of us start thinking about speaking our faith we become acutely embarrassed. Oh, nobody's going to fling us in jail, but they may make us feel odd or simply avoid us. So, though we're willing to recruit for the local church, the idea of talking to people about God is downright unnerving.

Yet think of all the people who are grinding out lives of quiet desperation, trapped in a kind of low-key unhappiness—unhappy at work, unhappy in marriage, strangely distraught. No wonder the *New York Times* now lists self-help books weekly; everybody seems to be searching for some new way to live. Well, what else does the gospel announce? Life! The good news is that there is a new way of life for us all. Think of being free from the tedious cycle of failure, self-help, and failure again. Think of being free to enjoy our neighbors without being bogged down by the burden of ourselves. More deeply, think of having a sense of the presence of God's love, built-in on a permanent basis. Now, the gospel says, now we can be free to *live* in Jesus Christ our Lord.

Are you ready for a mystery? All along, from the first day of creation, God has wanted us to be free, free for love. Why else is there a world if we are not to be together with God? No wonder God called Israel to be a holy people. No wonder God sent Jesus Christ among us. And we have been called to speak! Think of it; we speak not so that churches will grow, but so that God's own saving purposes will be fulfilled.

So let us stir up the evangelical Spirit we have been given. We must not be trapped in our own timidities, afraid of what people will think of us. No, through the centuries, Christians have put up with ridicule, jail, and even martyrdom for the sake of the gospel. Probably we can survive a little embarrassment! But speak we must. We tell news of a new order of life to be lived, free and loving and, yes, devout. We know whom we have believed; let us share good news with the world.

GOSPEL: LUKE 17:1–10

Here we have four separate teachings strung together, vv. 1–2, vv. 3–4, vv. 5–6, vv. 7–10. Luke has woven the teachings together in a sequence that flows with a kind of logic. Nevertheless, preachers may wish to divide the section, preaching on the teachings in vv. 1–6, or on the little parable about the servant in vv. 7–10. Let us take a look at the four teachings.

In vv. 1–4, we have words pertaining to our common life together in Christian community. There is a "Woe" (vv. 1–2) addressed to those who in their Christian freedom may inadvertently lead others astray (presumably "little ones" are weaker Christians). Discussions of "weaker" Christians to be found in 1 Corinthians 8 and Romans 14 will help us understand the teaching. Those who lead others into scandalous behavior will get what's coming to them (being dumped in the sea with a millstone around their necks would be nicer!). The teaching ends with a stern warning—Watch out!

Then, in vv. 3-4, we have a call to mutual correction and forgiveness among Christians. If someone wrongs us, we are to point out the wrong and, when they intend to change, forgive them. Forgiveness is stressed above all. The figure "seven times" should be understood as a metaphor for *unlimited* mercy. So, two teachings in vv. 1-4 fit together nicely. We must not lead others into temptation, but instead should live together with mutual correction, repentance, and unlimited forgiveness.

No wonder the disciples are stunned; "Increase our faith," they exclaim (v. 5). The demands of the common Christian life are almost overwhelming. Jesus answers with splendid hyperbole: Even a little faith can uproot a sycamore (which has an elaborate root system) and dump it into the sea. The saying, which shows up in different contexts in Mark and Matthew, must be preached with care. Sometimes Christians can tumble into magical thinking, or even into manipulative faith; v. 6 intends neither. God commands a common life that, truthfully, is beyond our capacity. After all, though we are Christian and thus forgiven sinners, we still struggle with our sins. How can we possibly not lead others astray or be slow to forgive? Verse 6 answers by pointing to our faith in God, saying that even the smallest degree of faith, which we do have, will make the common Christian life possible. In faith we know God's will for our lives, in faith we realize we have been forgiven, and in faith we share a common, enabling Spirit.

The little parable that follows (vv. 7-10) may also relate to the Christian life. See how the parable works. At the start of the parable we are in a position of dominance; we have someone working for us who is both a farmhand and a domestic slave. In effect, we are the boss. When you have someone doing a job for you, do you cater to your worker? "Come on in, sit down, use my slippers, watch my television. May I fix you a drink? Here let me serve you supper!" The parable finds this appalling: Do you reward people with special gratitude for doing what they are *supposed* to be doing?

Then, suddenly, without warning, the parable flips us out of our in-charge position: "You, when you have done all that is commanded you, say, 'We are simply servants; we have done no more than our duty.'" Notice that the *action* of the parable is part of its message; it tips us out of a position of mastery into a modest view of ourselves. We are servants doing what God expects of us and, therefore, need not lay claim to extra "brownie points." If we preach a sermon on the parable, the design of the sermon should incorporate the same sort of radical role reversal.

Does the parable connect with the teachings? Perhaps. The only way we will ever be able to forgive others or to show concern for over-scrupulous Christians is to be displaced. We are not the center of a universe surrounded by others who, we suppose, should serve our needs. No, we are people of God who are *supposed* to love and serve neighbors. In faith, relying on God's helping Spirit, we can live together gracefully.

The Twenty-first Sunday after Pentecost

Lutheran	Roman Catholic	Episcopal	Common Lectionary
Ruth 1:1–19a	2 Kings 5:14–17	Ruth 1:(1–7) 8–19a	Mic. 1:2; 2:1–10
2 Tim. 2:8–13	2 Tim. 2:8–13	2 Tim. 2:(3–7) 8–15	2 Tim. 2:8–15
Luke 17:11–19	Luke 17:11–19	Luke 17:11–19	Luke 17:11–19

FIRST LESSON: RUTH 1:1–19a

The story of Ruth is often labeled a novella. While it is not a long story—only four short chapters—it is designed artfully with discipline, economy, and restraint. The book is the story of Ruth, a Moabite woman, and Naomi, her Jewish mother-in-law.

If we wish to preach a story, above all we must define episodes clearly. The story begins in the third person with what sounds almost like a fairy-tale start, "In the days when the Judges ruled . . ." Famine in the land has propelled Elimelech, his wife Naomi, and their two sons on a trek to the more fertile land of Moab. Their prosperity is short-lived; Elimelech dies, leaving Naomi to care for her two sons. The boys take Moabite wives, Orpah and Ruth. Then, again tragedy strikes. After ten years, the childless marriages are shattered; both sons die. Poor Naomi, a victim of stark tragedy, is left in an alien male-dominated land with her two Moabite daughters-in-law.

Now the action begins, and we focus on Naomi. She has heard that famine is over and there is once more food in Judah. So she turns back to her homeland. (The word "return" echoes again and again throughout the narrative, signaling a major theme.) What is she to do with her two daughters-in-law? "Go return each of you to her mother's house. May the Lord deal kindly with you, as you have dealt with the dead and with me. The Lord grant that you may find a home, each of you in the house of her husband!" The phrase "her mother's house" is remarkable in a male-dominated society, but it may imply "your real mothers" and not Naomi, a mere mother-in-law. More remarkable is the fact that Naomi draws an analogy between the tender fidelity of the two *Moabite* women and the Lord. Of course, what Naomi suggests is practical. Three lone women have no place in a male-dominated society; the young women must return, remarry, and find security in the house of a husband.

Ruth and Orpah balk at the advice: "No, we will return with you to your people." So Naomi parades a scathing logic: "Have I more sons in my womb to become husbands for you? Turn back, my daughters. . . ." Orpah succumbs to hard logic; she kisses Naomi goodbye, and quite reasonably chooses to return to Moab. Now the story is reduced to two characters, Naomi and Ruth.

When Naomi again bids Ruth to return to her Moabite family and her Moabite God, the young woman answers in a famous speech:

Do not force me to leave you,
    To turn back from following you.
For wherever you go, I will go;
    Where you stay, I will stay.
Your people are my people;
    Your God is now my God.

She even invokes the name of Yahweh in a loyalty oath (v. 17b). Naomi, seeing Ruth's strange determination, is silent. The episode ends as the two women journey on to Bethlehem.

We must not dismiss the story of Ruth as a product of Jewish triumphalism, designed to celebrate a return to Judah and to Yahweh from alien Moabite territory. The story is radical. Remarkably, Naomi sees in her Moabite daughters-in-law an image of the kindness *(hesed)* of Yahweh. Still more astonishing, Ruth's great declaration is a mirror of God's covenant fidelity—"I will be your God and you will be my people." The story reaches beyond religious exclusiveness.

But we should not fail to notice courage in the story. Naomi, as beset by trouble as was Job, responds bravely. She turns back to Judah when God favors the land with food. And she has the boldness to go alone, sending her daughters-in-law back to their families. In spite of her bitterness (see vv. 20–21), she is willing to sacrifice herself in love. Of course, Ruth is also courageous. Wisely, Orpah has chosen a proper course for her life; she returns to the security of home with some chance for a future with her people and her God. The story in no way denigrates Orpah's actions. But Ruth's faithful love for Naomi leads her beyond prudence. She is willing to risk herself in a society that scarcely favors unmarried women, to go as an alien to Judah, to renounce her family and her gods and, in a binding oath, to speak the name of Yahweh. Of course, she is already a proper follower of the Lord because she has demonstrated love and covenant loyalty.

Perhaps the real actor in the story is unseen, although not unmentioned. Subtly, the name of Lord has been introduced all through the narrative (see vv. 6, 8, 9, 13, 16, 17). Through human choices, all along God has been choosing. Through human faithfulness, God's own faithful favor has shone. The theology of Ruth is cautious; God does not manipulate. Nevertheless, in and through all things, the providence of God is a determined, loving, moving presence. The God of covenant faithfulness is furthering human covenants and endorsing human lives in order to bring about an ultimate return. Preachers must not moralize: Naomi struggles with self-pity and Ruth may well be rash. No, the real story within the story of Ruth is of the unfailing providence of God, a God whose name is Love.

The separate scenes in the story are easy to demark: (1) The tragic situation; (2) Naomi's advice to her daughters-in-law; (3) Orpah's response; (4) Ruth's vow. In each of the episodes there is theological meaning, and it is important that the tale not be turned into a psychological study or a soap opera. We can preach as if we were hearing, understanding, and considering the story, episode by episode. But remember, the real story is a story of God.

Perhaps the way to preach the passage would be to set up different points of view. We could begin a sermon looking at the situation as the Bible does, from a third-person perspective. We might then listen to Naomi's advice through the consciousness of Orpah, a sane and quite practical woman. Then, we could seek to understand Ruth's astonishing vow through Naomi's surprise. Finally, we could back off and suddenly view everything that has happened as a story of God-with-us, which of course it is. The story of Ruth is a story of the covenant faithfulness of God.

Common Lectionary: Micah 1:2; 2:1–10. Here is another choice, a passage from Micah. The passage contains a prophecy against social evil and, of all things, the voicing of a rather familiar complaint from the prophet's audience—preachers should stick to positive thinking, and quit spouting negative pulpit threats.

Micah 1:2 sets a scene; God is presenting a case in some heavenly court for all the people of earth to hear (cf. 6:1). What is God's complaint? God is out of patience with those who foreclose on the property of others (2:2). Because they have power, they will dream plans for evil at night and then, in the morning, get up and do what they have devised (2:1). According to the prophet, God is dreaming up a just reward for the wicked, so that they will end up crying, "We are utterly ruined!" (2:3-4) The wicked are covetous and thus are violating God's commandment: You shall not covet. They shall lose what they have gained—they shall be humbled (2:3c), their property shall be redistributed (2:4b), and they will have no public standing (2:5). The wicked may plot evil but, look out, God is counterplotting!

Micah 2:6-11 is difficult to interpret, in part because of textual problems. Verses 6-7 represent the complaints of Micah's audience, in effect, "Don't preach to *us*! You prophets shouldn't speak such things! Our God is not short-tempered. No, God favors the morally upright (like ourselves)!" The audience seems to be saying, "Stick to the gospel, preacher, and quit meddling." Verses 8-10 give voice to the prophet's reply: "You are the enemy of the people." He details how they have oppressed the trusting poor; they evict families (2:9), saying, "Get out of your homes" (2:10a).

Finally, Micah adds sheer irony in v. 11: You people want a "spiritual preacher," he says, who will make you feel good about partying (literally, "preach to you of beer and wine"). A gospel of celebration will always be welcome!

The passage is startlingly contemporary. Do not most American congregations crave a feel-good gospel? A gospel for "be (happy) attitudes"? We seem to want sermons that can be crammed onto a tiny lapel button: "Smile, God loves you." What we don't want to hear is any criticism of American national policy or unrestrained American capitalism. But the trouble is that the gospel of God's mercy can only be heard at the cross where all our sins, and emphatically our social sins, are shown up. We cannot be reconciled to God unless we are willing to go along with God's just will. Certainly God has willed a covenant community in which there is mutual regard and compassion. Profiteering at the expense of others, though viewed by many as normal business practice, is never *good* business to God.

The passage in Micah is amazingly perceptive. Perhaps evil does begin in fantasy, in the dreams of domination we all harbor. Wasn't it a little child who confessed truthfully, "In all my dreams I'm someone big, bigger than anybody"? Our dreams, big dreams, are pushed along by advertising that fans our desires. And, before you know it, we're up and about trying to possess our desires, even though others may be deprived.

Nevertheless, God is still God, and God's covenant purposes will be fulfilled. Though we may scheme, God's own dream ultimately shall be realized. Thus, we may expect our unlimited desires to be thwarted. After all, though we affirm the love of God, let us remember that God's love is "tough love," tough enough to save us.

If we preach the passage, perhaps we will have to begin where we are, with our own strange propensity for evil. How easily we can tumble into sin; it begins with our daydreaming. We have such big dreams! In all our dreams we get somewhere, or have something, or are somebody—almost always, unfortunately, at the expense of others. Sadly, every now and then our dreams take over, and we do evil. We try to put a good face on it, label it "shrewd business," or a matter of "national security," but the truth is that getting what we want usually involves harming others, yes, even other nations.

What does God say, according to Micah? God says to us, "You will be ruined!" For God will not tolerate power politics if it means poverty for other nations. And emphatically God will not put up with our getting rich at the expense of others. God is dreaming of a world where all the children of earth can live together, sharing, serving, and trading love for love. If our dreams lead us up against God's dream, then ruin is inevitable.

Well, we don't want to hear that sort of message in our churches, do we? Isn't Christian faith supposed to make us feel good? We love Jesus; we said so when once we joined a church. How can God turn against us Jesus People? The God we worship is "full of mercy, and slow to anger"; the Bible says so. Preachers ought to loosen up a bit and help us to celebrate the sweet mercies of God.

Look, God loves us, sure enough. But if we love God, we must love God's dream for the world as well. Love isn't merely a feeling, it's going along with God in *God's* way. And we have been shown God's way in the love of Christ. So now God calls us to change our ways—no more power politics, no more shrewd business, no more "coveting" dreams at the expense of neighbors. How can we repent? Why, by loving our neighbors in the Lord!

SECOND LESSON: 2 TIMOTHY 2:8–13

Form critics have helped us to read Scripture. Here is a passage that begins with a quoted creed (v. 8) and ends with another quote, perhaps

The Twenty-first Sunday after Pentecost 17

of a hymn stanza (vv. 11b–13). Although it would be possible to preach the hymn by itself, the whole passage is quite wonderful.

The unknown author of 2 Timothy imagines Paul in prison urging young Timothy to be faithful. In v. 8, Paul quotes a familiar two-part confession of faith: "Remember Jesus Christ," he cries, "risen from the dead, descended from David . . ." Notice the form of the confession, ascending and descending, not unlike the formula found at the beginning of Romans (1:3–4). "My gospel!" Paul exclaims, endorsing the confession of faith.

For the sake of the gospel, Paul is willing to be chained like a criminal (v. 9). The word "criminal" here is unusual and appears only in Luke 23:33–34, 39, where it refers to the two men who were crucified with Christ. But though the apostle is chained like a common crook, he gleefully announces, "Not that God's word is chained!" Persecution, instead of restricting the gospel, may actually amplify good news.

Paul says that he can put up with anything. He will endure suffering so that the people whom God has picked out for liberation may be set free and anticipate reunion (glory) with the risen Christ.

Then 2 Timothy drops in another quote, an absolutely wonderful lyric hymn:

> If we died with him, we shall also live with him,
> If we endure, we shall also rule with him,
> If we deny, [that one] will also deny us,
> If we are faithless, [that one] stays faithful,
>   for he cannot contradict himself.

The first two lines of the hymn are parallel and full of promise. The third line, which may include a reference to Matt. 10:33, is also a parallel construction. But the last line is splendidly offbeat; parallel syntax blows up. For how can God deny God's own covenant fidelity? Once more, we are surprised by grace!

The hymn should not surprise us. Though the cross surely shows up our infidelities—we deny, desert, and betray our Lord; nevertheless, God is faithful and, in the risen Christ, returns to us, reaffirming covenant love. Only Christian faith could write such an offbeat, astonishing lyric.

Notice that the first short confession of faith (v. 8) is the basis for the final coda (vv. 11b–13). In between, the author of Timothy has Paul in chains affirming the sheer liberating power of the gospel, a gospel that, based on Jesus Christ, trusts the faithful love of God. The supposition

"If we are faithless . . ." gets a surprise conclusion that reaches into the profound mystery of God's love.

How can we preach the passage and pull off some of the same surprise we find in the last line of the hymn? (1) We can begin by being honest about the Christian life; it isn't easy. We may not end up in jail, as Paul did, but we're bound to struggle. The world worships power, but we stand for peace. Our jobs frequently demand "toughness," but we are committed to compassion. In our world, the Christian life means a constant tension. (2) But hear the good news! If we give up the way of the world and follow Christ, we will *live*. We will no longer be trapped in the destructiveness of our age, we will be free, and glad, and good. (3) What's more, we can look forward to a life beyond life with Jesus Christ the Lord. He was crucified by the world. But, God has raised him up. Though it may sound like old-time religion, there's something in most of us that responds to the promises: "We shall live. We shall reign with him!" (4) Well, what if we balk? What if we are faithless? We frequently are. We know what we deserve. Wasn't it Luther who said that if he were God and the world treated him as it has treated God, he would have kicked the world to pieces long ago! (5) Surprise, listen to the word of Scripture: "If we are faithless [God] stays faithful." God cannot deny God's own nature! God doesn't hand out mercy, God *is* mercy. "Forgive them," cried Christ on the cross. (6) Now do you see why we want to struggle to live a Christian life? Not to cash in on a heavenly payoff, no, but in astonished gratitude to be faithful to a God who is always faithful in love.

GOSPEL: LUKE 17:11–19

The story of the ten lepers seems to echo the healing of Naaman in 2 Kings 5. When Naaman was healed, though he was an alien, he turned back to give thanks to the God of Israel. In Luke, the story follows the abrupt parable of the "unworthy servant." If the servant parable tells us to do what we are supposed to do, the story of the lepers seems to say that mere obedience without grateful worship is insufficient.

The lepers are living in the DMZ between Samaria and Galilee. Though "leprosy" in the Scriptures is clearly not Hansen's disease, nevertheless it was some sort of contagious skin eruption; lepers were kept at a distance (Num. 5:1–4). Like beggars everywhere, they cry out for help, "Jesus, Master, have pity!" Jesus answers with an abrupt command (scarcely a Pastoral Care approach), "Go," he says, adding, "Show yourselves to the priests." The command is in accordance with the law of Moses (Leviticus 13—14).

On their way, Luke remarks, "It so happened that they were healed."

One of those healed, a Samaritan, returns to glorify God and to thank Jesus. Verses 15b–16 contain three phrases—"fell at [his] feet," "praising," and "giving [him] thanks"—which in the Greek of Luke-Acts are all usual terms for worship. Then, with a touch of irony, Jesus asks, "Were not ten cleansed? Where are the nine?" Obviously, they are off doing the law. So the passage seems to be telling us that faith is both obedience and grateful worship. "Your faith has made you whole," says Jesus (v. 19). The Greek *sesōken,* which the RSV translates "well" (lit. "saved"), is better translated as "whole."

The story is scarcely consistent history. If Jesus dispatches the lepers to do the law, for example, why does he blame them for not returning? But history is not the primary purpose of the passage. The story is theological: Doing the law is good, but mere obedience is an insufficient response to the saving power of God; we must fall down in worship with praise and thanksgiving *(eucharistia).*

Luke has a secondary theme that is picked up parenthetically in vv. 16b and 18. The one who returns is a "Samaritan," which in Luke seems to be a code word for Gentile. Luke, addressing Gentile Christians, wants to hold up an example of true faith by a non-Jew.

Luther was asked to define true worship. He answered, "The tenth leper turning back." The essence of Christian worship is gratitude. We give thanks for all that God has done in our lives. Of course, worship without the obedience of faith can turn into a pious form of religious perversion. Likewise, obedience without worship will become tedious moralism in no time. Most congregations these days seem to be at odds over the two options. Is Christian faith action or piety? The story of the ten lepers in Luke seems to be saying that a "whole" Christian life includes both; we serve by doing God's will *and* giving grateful praise.

The passage can be preached within a narrative structure. (1) We can picture the ten lepers in a row, begging, "Jesus, Master, have pity on us!" Their cry is altogether human. Most of us at wit's end find ourselves inwardly calling out to God. (2) How does Jesus answer? Of all things, with a command—"Go!" Again and again, when we come hustling up to God full of our own anguish, God issues a command; go, love, do. (3) The lepers did as they were told in an act of faith. We think of faith as believing, or perhaps as a warm-tub God feeling in our hearts. But in the Bible, faith is a venture. (4) If faith is no more than obedience, it can turn into leaden moralism—doing the rules! (5) See, one of the lepers returned to give praise. Christian worship is always thanksgiving for God's good grace. (6) Now do you understand what "wholeness" is? The Christian life is not merely doing the words of Jesus. No, we worship, giving thanks for our salvation in Christ Jesus. Worship *and* obedience come together in faith.

The story of the ten lepers is a Christian call to worship.

The Twenty-second Sunday after Pentecost

Lutheran	Roman Catholic	Episcopal	Common Lectionary
Gen. 32:22–30	Exod. 17:8–13	Gen. 32:3–8, 22–30	Hab. 1:1–3; 2:1–4
2 Tim. 3:14—4:5	2 Tim. 3:14—4:2	2 Tim. 3:14—4:5	2 Tim. 3:14—4:5
Luke 18:1–8a	Luke 18:1–8	Luke 18:1–8a	Luke 18:1–8

FIRST LESSON: GENESIS 32:22–30

The famous story of Jacob wrestling an angel may originally have been a folktale about a river demon who was attempting to prevent Jacob from crossing a stream. In childhood, most of us heard stories about trolls that lurked beneath bridges and leapt upon unsuspecting travelers. The story of Jacob, however, has been rewritten into a theological understanding of God's good purposes. Some scholars suggest that vv. 25b, 26b, 28–29, and 31b–32 contain later rewriting, but such speculation is hard to pin down because the sources were formed gradually into one story.

The tale is often preached as a conversion in which Jacob, by heart-wrestling his own soul, becomes a new person. More often, the story is probed psychologically; frightened Jacob struggles with his own weighty guilts and finally pins down some forgiveness. But such gambits obscure theology. Though the story is multilayered—explaining the name "Israel" (v. 28), telling the origin of the word "Peniel" (v. 30), and giving reason for an ancient dietary law (v. 32)—its real meaning is theological. The story of Jacob at the river Jabbok is a story of God's covenant promises and thus of God's dealing with Jacob through whom promises will be fulfilled.

The story begins with Jacob, a "mother's boy" and a cheat, afraid to face his brother, Esau (vv. 6–12). Having sent his wives and children over the river, Jacob is alone in the night. Suddenly, someone leaps on him and the two wrestle. The contest appears to be a draw, so the unknown assailant begs to halt the match—"Let me go, for the day is breaking."

(Evil spirits in ancient folktales often attack at night but lose power in daylight.) Jacob presses his advantage, "I will not let you go until you bless me"; he asks for some sharing of supernatural power. So far, the story fits the pattern of the troll under a bridge.

Notice that an overlay of theology has transformed the tale. "What is your name?" asks the mysterious wrestler. Jacob confesses his name, which means "cheat" (see 25:26; 27:36). To know a name is to know *identity:* Jacob's identity has been "cheat," for he diddled his brother Esau and fleeced his father-in-law Laban. But now Jacob is renamed Israel, which is explained as "He who strives with God" (although, literally, Israel means "God rule.") Then, brashly, Jacob asks, "Tell me, I pray, your name." But the mysterious wrestler significantly does not disclose a name. Instead, Jacob is given a blessing.

Then Jacob names the place Peniel ("face of God"): "For I have seen God face to face, and have lived!" The sun rises and Jacob crosses the river, limping because his thigh had been touched.

The episode of Jacob wrestling on a riverbank is inserted in the midst of the story of his return home to face Esau and, in a sense, the episode may be seen as a preparation for a glad reconciliation of the two brothers (Genesis 33). But a broader context is the story of God's covenant promise. God has picked out Jacob, a thoroughgoing con artist, as an instrument of the divine will. Through Israel (nee Jacob), the offspring of Abraham will be many; God will have a people. No wonder Jacob is renamed. Though a "cheat," he will play a decisive role in the ruling purpose of God.

Of course, in a way, the dramatic episode at the river Jabbok is a parable of God and Israel. Surely the Hebrew Scriptures from start to finish chronicle God's continual wrestling with Israel (and with us). From the beginning, in covenant love, God made a people for communion. So, all along, God must wrestle with our willfulness, and prepare us for reconciliation. How can we fallen human beings be renamed "children of God"?

Jacob is changed. Visited by the unnamed presence of God, Jacob is a different man. Yes, he will limp. But, though crippled, he does become honorable, indeed reconcilable. Notice, however, that transformation is *not* a condition of Jacob's relationship to God; no, God chose him while his name was appropriately "cheat." (Remember, "God shows love for us in that while we were yet sinners . . ." Rom. 5:8.) With God and in God's purpose, Jacob is transformed.

The story is dramatic, and the structure of a sermon must be equally dramatic. We must not enter the consciousness of Jacob lest the sermon become a psychological study in conversion and the profound theological themes be lost. No, in the wrestling we must see God struggling to bring about a new reconciling people. And, somehow, we must indicate that God's election of Jacob, a cheat, is part of an eternal purpose for the world. We probably will design a sermon that will move along much as do the episodes in the story. But we will speak as if we and a congregation are hearing the story and thinking it out all at once, thus allowing for theological reflection. There is an underlying theological movement to the story that we can trace and use in a sermon.

Out of all people, God picked Jacob. Remember how Jacob connived with his mother to steal his brother Esau's birthright, and think of how Jacob shrewdly tricked his own father-in-law out of a flock of fine sheep. His name, Jacob, means "cheat," and he was well named! But God seems to have a long record of choosing sinners, perhaps because that's all there is in our human world.

So God must wrestle with us. We are rebellious people and, somehow, God must pin us down and change our lives. We don't want to serve God's will, and we certainly don't want to be reconciled with our brothers and sisters on earth. Perhaps the story of our lives is a struggle with God.

Of course, God will not yield. Unseen, but unceasing, God will reshape our lives. To us the struggle may seem agonizing, and even crippling, but God will free us from ourselves. Jacob was wounded, and yet became whole.

See the result. Jacob is a different man. He goes out to meet his brother Esau. No more tricks, no sneaky evasions; he is able to be reconciled to his brother and to God. He even sets up an altar on the land.

Now you see what happened in the night by the river Jabbok. Jacob was given a new name by God, a new name and a new character. Now he is called Israel, for he has struggled with God and been changed. Through Israel, God will keep the ancient covenant promise, "I will be your God. You will be my people."

The story of Jacob is a story of God's saving grace.

Common Lectionary: Habakkuk 1:1–3; 2:1–4. We have previously explored this passage from Habakkuk (see discussion under the Twentieth Sunday after Pentecost).

SECOND LESSON: 2 TIMOTHY 3:14—4:5

Well, when it comes to "itching ears," "collecting teachers to suit our own likings" and "wandering into myths," we twentieth-century Christians may be in a class by ourselves. Any preacher who would speak to us will have to stand firm in the gospel. Listen to the words of Paul the apostle as reported by 2 Timothy: "I charge you in the presence of God and of Jesus Christ who is to judge the living and the dead . . . preach the word. . . ." Paul's shivery, solemn speech falls on us as a great commission—on *all* of us, ordained and unordained alike. For we who are the church are surely called to preach and teach, to convince, convict and exhort, in season and out of season, patiently. How are we to keep our heads and do the work of an evangelist nowadays?

Paul sends us back to our roots. "Stick with what you have learned and have firmly believed," he says (3:14). Thus, he points us to the gospel message. But then, he urges us to remember from whom we have heard the gospel, and to recall the Scriptures that have shaped our faith. Timothy has received the gospel from his grandmother and his mother (2 Tim. 1:5) and, of course, from his mentor Paul (3:10–11), people who have shown him the true character of Christian charity and courage. But Timothy has also been taught by the Scriptures, Scriptures that have judged, corrected, and trained him in faith (3:16). Paul begins by urging Timothy to stand firmly in the gospel message. Only then does he turn to discuss personal witness and the testimony of the Scriptures. Martin Luther insisted that the church was a *worthaus*, a word house rather than a library; faith is usually heard before it is studied in Scripture. The gospel spreads by word of mouth and only later is scribbled down on pages.

Second Timothy 3:16 has been bandied about as support for biblical authority and in particular for the notion of verbal inspiration. The verse, however, is exceedingly difficult to translate, much less interpret. Do we read "all scripture" or "every scripture" (i.e., some particular passages in Scripture)? Do we translate "inspired" as a qualifying modifier or as a general description ("every God-inspired scripture is . . ." or "every scripture is inspired by God . . .")? The term "inspired" (Greek *theopneustos*, lit. "God-spirited") appears nowhere else in the Bible. Let us attempt to clarify the verse that, at the time when the Timothys were written, almost certainly referred specifically to the Hebrew Scriptures, and not to the Gospels and epistles that are included in our Bibles today. The term "inspired" is scarcely an exclusive term; all kinds of edifying words were considered "of the spirit" in the life of the early church. The verse seems to be saying that, by the Spirit, the Scriptures are useful to Christian people who have faith in Christ and are being-saved.

A sermon on the passage could probably begin with the cultural problem Timothy faced. How do you speak to people with "itching ears"? Certainly, we can understand the problem. Nowadays people seem to be church-hoppers, shopping around for congenial religion. Give us a mellow gospel, please, positive thinking, possibility thinking, Jungian symbols, or PTL hoopla. With churches competing in the religious marketplace for a quota of souls to save, the temptation to tailor the gospel to popular tastes is extreme.

Yet, watch out, we preach in the presence of God! We do not merely peddle a gospel as church promotion. No, we preach of God in the presence of God. No wonder Paul lays a heavy charge on young Timothy! In God's presence the question of *truth* is paramount. We do not ask, What sells? We do not rate our words by the number of "bus-'em-in" pew sitters we can cram in our churches. No, we must ask, Is our gospel true to God in whose presence we preach?

So we must hold on to the gospel we have heard. The good news has been preached down through the ages from first-century Jerusalem to Greek marketplaces, in Roman forums and feudal cities, in Luther's castle church and Calvin's Geneva, across the sweep of the American frontier, and, yes, to us. Always the good news has been filled with talk of Jesus Christ, the man who was crucified, whom God raised up. There's a pulpit in New England, carved with words on the preacher's side. They read: "Preach Jesus Christ and him crucified." We should recall the gospel message we have heard.

How can we be sure of the gospel we preach? See, the good news changes lives! The gospel has set people free. Isn't there an old story about a clergyman who, challenged to prove the truth of the gospel, paraded in fifty folk who were willing to testify that their lives had been altogether changed by news of Jesus Christ? What certifies the gospel? Human lives, new lives. We've seen such people; they have spoken God to us.

Of course, there is also the witness of Scripture. We can turn to the Bible, where the gospel of the first apostles found its way into print. The first-century world was different. Christians then spoke a different language; they faced quite different problems. But in Scripture, on almost every page, you find a story of God-with-us from creation to Christ, a story that still makes sense of life.

Our job is speaking: All of us are the ministry of Jesus Christ. We speak in a troubled age when people want meaning, but often on their own terms. The only way we can get the gospel straight is to preach the word that fills the Scriptures and gives new life, the word of Jesus Christ, God-with-us. What does Paul say to Timothy? "Stick to the gospel," he says—good advice for us.

GOSPEL: LUKE 18:1–8

Here is a little parable that is tugged in different directions by its context. The first verse introduces the parable under the topic heading of prayer; we are to pray at all times. But, in the last verse, there is mention of God's coming judgment and human faith. Some scholars suppose that vv. 2–5(6) are an original parable. Verses 1 and 7–8, then, are different interpretations that have been tied onto the story. What on earth does the parable mean?

The parable has two characters, a judge and a widow. The widow was a stock character in stories. In addition to orphans and aliens, widows are singled out in the Hebrew Scriptures as objects of special care. God is a God who protects widows (Deut. 10:18; Ps. 68:5; 146:9). Israel, like God, is to offer extra protection to widows, although, according to the prophets, such concern was frequently neglected. The widow was a helpless figure in a male-dominated culture. While widows could live off the estates of their husbands (legally, they could not inherit), in fact they were often destitute. No welfare system provided for them. There was only social obligation under God's law.

The judge is described as a man who has neither reverence for God nor respect for others; he is evidently a corrupt judge living among affluent urbanites. There are scriptural passages that urge judges to emulate the justice of God (2 Chron. 19:6–7) and, in particular, to show special concern for the rights of widows. But, in the parable, the judge totally ignored the pleading of the widow who cried, "Settle [vindicate] my case."

Notice that the character of the judge does not change; he is not contrite, converted, or moved with pity. A stinker at the beginning of the parable, he is still a stinker at the end of the parable. Nevertheless, bugged by the woman, he gives in; "She will wear me down," he says, exasperated. He is ruled by self-interest to the last.

But, remember, the Bible regards God as a good judge who always hears the prayers of widows: "[God] will not ignore . . . the widow when she pours out her story. . . . The prayer of the humble pierces the clouds. . . . And the Lord will not delay" (Sir. 35:12–18). Evidently, the parable operates on a logic of "but how much more." If a crook will give in to being badgered, God, who is eager to hear the cries of the oppressed, will respond *at once*. Thus v. 8a seems to fit the parable.

What about v. 1, the injunction "always to pray and not lose heart"? Well, if God wants to hear prayers and to respond quickly, we need not nag God. We can, however, pray on all occasions with confidence and trust; God is just, God is good.

The parable in Luke appears immediately after a section on the coming of the kingdom (17:20–37). When will the kingdom come? The answer is that the kingdom will come without warning when God chooses. Disciples are to watch and pray faithfully, unlike people in the days of Noah or Lot. Verse 8b gathers the parable into the same discourse. Though disciples may be discouraged and, indeed, be weary of faithful praying in an oppressive time, nevertheless God's promises shall be. God is a good judge who will vindicate the oppressed.

At a time when Christians are discouraged and prayers stammer, the parable of the widow and the crooked judge is encouraging. All we have to do is to see in Christ Jesus a different kind of judge; he died for us and, risen, works for the cause of his own. The parable addresses a weary Christian people who wonder why the world remains unjust in spite of all their praying.

A sermon might begin with a depiction of our unjust and troubled world. Then, we might wonder if our prayers do any good at all—is God deaf? Well, all Jesus hands us is the image of a persistent widow and a corrupt judge. But, hold on, our God is a *good* judge. ("Forgive them," cried Christ from the cross.) We can be sure that, ultimately, God will bring about a new order of justice and love. So, we pray with assurance, trusting the wisdom of God—and the mercy.

The Twenty-third Sunday after Pentecost

Lutheran	Roman Catholic	Episcopal	Common Lectionary
Deut. 10:12–22	Sir. 35:12–14, 16–17	Jer. 14:(1–6), 7–10, 19–22	Zeph. 3:1–9
2 Tim. 4:6–8, 16–18	2 Tim. 4:6–8, 16–18	2 Tim. 4:6–8, 16–18	2 Tim. 4:6–8, 16–18
Luke 18:9–14	Luke 18:9–14	Luke 18:9–14	Luke 18:9–14

FIRST LESSON: DEUTERONOMY 10:12–22

The passage is a great summary of the message of Deuteronomy. In ten brief verses, we are handed a theology.

Notice that the passage appears after a long recital of God's goodness to Israel in the past (9:1—10:11). Again and again, according to Moses, God has forgiven stubborn, unbelieving Israel (9:4–7). God gave the law, but Israel chased around a golden calf (9:9–19); God gave the land, yet Israel never trusted God's promises (9:22—10:5). Though Israel has repeatedly been rebellious, God has always been faithful.

After a long look at the past, Moses sets forth a kind of credo for Israel. Verse 12, which sounds remarkably like Mic. 6:8, begins, "Now Israel, what does the Lord your God require of you, but to fear the Lord your God, to walk in all [God's] ways, to love [and] to serve the Lord your God. . . ." The verse echoes material from earlier chapters of Deuteronomy (chaps. 5, 6). Verse 13 is explicit; we serve God by keeping "commandments and statutes." Together vv. 12–13 recall the giving of the commandments at Sinai.

Verses 14–15 are a confession of faith in God who is sovereign over the heavens and the earth and yet who, in love, freely came to make covenant with Israel.

How can Israel respond to God's unmerited grace? "Circumcise the foreskin of your heart," advises Moses (v. 16). The metaphor (perhaps from Jer. 4:4) is aptly chosen, for in Israel circumcision had become a sign of the covenant. But covenant fidelity involves ethics. As usual, ethical obedience is argued from the nature of God. As God is fair and will not be bribed, so Israel must be just. As God cares for the orphan and the widow and the stranger, so Israel must do likewise (vv. 17–19).

Then the passage returns to praise God, God who like a mighty warrior has been Israel's strength, doing "great and terrible things" (see Exod. 15:3). In v. 22, the passage concludes by recalling the deliverance from Egypt and the establishment of Israel, all as a sign of God's covenant faithfulness.

We can preach the passage by rearranging the argument. Perhaps a sermon could begin with a kind of amazement. When we speak the word "God," surely we mean a God who has the whole wide world in hand: To God "belong heaven and the heavens beyond heaven, the earth and everything in the earth" (v. 14).

"And yet. . . ." The words are full of surprise! The high and holy Lord God loves us little human creatures. That God should pick us out as a special people is astonishing. The famous couplet, "How odd of God/To choose the Jews," can be recited by us all. How amazing that God should choose us! We are all recipients of free covenant love.

Of course, we'll have to admit that God's love is undeserved. The human race hasn't shown much in the way of a moral track record; evil seems intractable. Yet again and again God has been merciful. God has liberated us from oppression and, in spite of our chronic rebelliousness, has shown patient mercy.

How do we respond? In love, of course. We must be God's people—a loving, trusting, faithful people. Wasn't it a famous British preacher who actually hauled a huge heavy cross into his pulpit and exclaimed: "See what God has done for us! Can we hold back?" From the first day of creation, to the escape from Egypt, to the high cross on calvary, see all that God has done. How do we respond? We give our hearts to God.

But, look out, don't forget ethics! Christian faith isn't merely a habit of the heart. Love is *always* a doing! Just as God has created a fine, fair world for us, filled with food for our hungers, so we must better the world for neighbors and share food with the hungry. As God has cared for enslaved Israel, so we must live for our neighbor's freedoms. As God in Christ has died to give us life, so we must be willing to die for others.

Such a sermon might properly end, as does the passage, by once more rehearsing the goodness of God in praise.

Common Lectionary: Zephaniah 3:1-9. This is a different passage, an oracle of woe (vv. 1-8). By adding v. 9 to the oracle, the lection ends with the promise of a new creation beyond the judgment of Judah. Many of the verses in the passage seem to echo words of Jeremiah.

Verses 1-2 set the tone of the oracle. Judah is rebellious: It will heed no voice (the prophets?) and accept no correction (the Deuteronomic reforms?). Judah will not turn to the Lord. Verses 3-4 are quite specific, documenting the general accusation. Four different groups are singled out: leaders—roaring lions; judges—scavenger wolves; prophets—shallow chatterers; and priests—lawless profaners. Verse 5 contrasts the Lord's fidelity with the infidelity of Judah: God gives constancy to life day after day, but God's people by contrast are shamefully unfaithful.

Verses 6-7 are strangely incredulous (and also difficult to translate). Look, says God, I have destroyed nations all around Judah; surely you'd think Judah would catch on and be corrected—but no, it is even more eager for corruption. God is lifting a divine eyebrow at Judah's intransigent stupidity.

Verse 8 is a grinding, terrible vow. Just you wait! God says, and goes on to predict the demise not only of Judah but of the world: "All the earth shall be burnt up!" A grim picture of judgment indeed.

Then, suddenly, there's v. 9. The verse is not a cop-out, but a promise that beyond inevitable destruction the human enterprise will have a new beginning. Note that the verse clearly picks up an image of Babel (Gen. 11:1-9). In the story of Babel, a rebellious human world fell into chaos when language was confused. Now God promises a new start for the world: "I will change the speech of the peoples to a pure speech." With common understanding, all together, the whole world will worship God and do God's perfect will.

The problem in preaching a passage such as this is that we are tempted to close the book on vv. 1-8, and to suppose that the church *is* the new creation; for, after all, isn't the story of Pentecost a fulfillment of v. 9?

Perhaps. But, obviously, our social order is still disfigured by political bombast, and by judges who may have little regard for the oppressed. As for the church, do we not have our share of shallow, windy preachers, not to mention pastors who by their sheer glibness may profane the sacred? Christian fulfillments cannot be allowed to erase the truth of the prophecy.

Nevertheless, the passage may call us to be who we are in Christ, namely, members of a new humanity. If we are new in Christ Jesus, then we must turn away from the old weariness of social sinfulness and embrace the ways and means of God's new order. Zephaniah still addresses our world, yes, *and* our churches.

A sermon may seem difficult to preach and, in a way, will be; we are dealing with a hard word of God. Perhaps the way to begin would be to look at history. All we have to do is to leaf the pages of our history books. The human story is a story of rising to power and tumbling into catastrophe. We speak of the great empires—the glory that was Greece, and then Rome, and then Germany, all gone. We strut across the stage only to stumble off into the wings. The pattern of rise and fall repeats itself so often that we have begun to think it is normal.

Zephaniah knows better; "God," he says. Why did Rome tumble into oblivion?—God! And why was Hitler's Germany brought low?—God! For the prophets see God as sovereign, ruling and overruling the human world. Oh, we should not think of God pulling puppet strings of disaster. No, we choose our own destructions in God's sight. Injustice breeds its revolutionary discontents; starvation its rages.

Maybe it is time to take a long honest look at our land. Zephaniah describes us well. Our leaders are bellicose; our courts are the playground of corporations. As for the church, can we be honest? We preach much idle chatter. We engage in gimmickry for worship in the sight of God's own holiness. Perhaps we are going to be a chapter in some ancient history book—the rise and fall of America.

Nevertheless, hear the good news. God's plans for the world are sure. Someday there will be a people with one Spirit who speak together with the deep, shared understanding of sisters and brothers. For in Jesus Christ God has given the world a new beginning, if we will but turn. Whatever may happen to us or our nation, God's promise is sure!

So how can we call our land back to God? Here we are the church of Jesus Christ in America. Our task is to announce the mercy of God so our neighbors may begin all over again in grace. Of course, we ourselves must change; we must speak honestly and worship in holiness. But our task is to speak God's name to America. God's name is justice, yes, and in Jesus Christ, mercy.

SECOND LESSON: 2 TIMOTHY 4:6-8, 16-18

Here the author of 2 Timothy portrays Paul, imprisoned and soon to die, writing an eloquent final word to Timothy.

Verse 6 is connected to v. 5 because both verses begin the same way ("As for you . . ."/"As for me . . ."). "As for me," says Paul, "I am already being poured out. . . ." He is using a metaphor of sacrifice, perhaps referring to the daily wine offering in the temple (see Num. 28:7). Evidently Paul sees that death ("the time of my departure") is coming, and is offering his death as self-sacrifice to God for the good of others (see 2 Mac. 6:28).

Then, in v. 7, we seem to have a string of athletic metaphors. "I have fought the good fight," seems to refer to a wrestling match; "I have finished the race," to a marathon; and "I have kept faith," possibly to an athlete's oath. In v. 8, Paul pictures his reward as a victor's wreath that he has won but not yet been publicly awarded. Paul will receive his recognition on "that day" (the day of judgment), along with all Christians who rejoice in Christ's appearing (lit. "epiphany"). Mention of "Christ's epiphany" at the end of v. 8 could mean "those who loved as a result of Christ's coming," but is more likely a reference to Christians who eagerly long for the second coming.

Verse 16 has occasioned some scholarly dispute. What is the meaning of "At my first defense . . ."? Though some scholars suppose that "first defense" refers to Paul's first stretch in prison, many others believe that here "defense" indicates some sort of preliminary court appearance that has been part of his second imprisonment. Though "everyone had deserted" Paul, his appearance in court gave him opportunity to proclaim the gospel to the Gentiles (v. 17). So, says Paul, "I was rescued from the lion's mouth," using a metaphor from Scripture (Ps. 22:21 and, of course, Dan. 6:20). But Paul knows that his deliverance is only a temporary stay of execution; his ultimate rescue will be safe passage to a "heavenly kingdom." He concludes with a final shout of praise, "To [God] be the glory for ever and ever. Amen."

If we preach the passage from 2 Timothy, we must not turn it into a history lesson by discussing Paul's different prison terms and final martyrdom. Preaching is a declaration of gospel and not a labored Bible study session. What 2 Timothy gives us is an imaginary last soliloquy from Paul to encourage us all to "be steady, endure suffering, and do the work of an evangelist" (v. 5). The passage is exemplary and not arcane history.

Preachers who preach the passage may wish to design an introduction for their sermons that can orient congregations to the passage. Old-fashioned melodramas often featured a final moving speech by an "I'm-about-to-die" kind of hero. Almost everyone in an audience would be dabbing at their eyes. And yet, those last speeches could stick in your mind; they could ennoble life. Whoever wrote 2 Timothy has written a speech for Paul. It may seem like melodrama but the words are moving. They speak to our Christian lives. Some such introduction may set up a sermon.

There are theological nuances tucked into the words of the passage. Notice that the metaphor of sacrifice is immediately transformed by the robust athletic allusions. A certain cloying self-pity can result from seeing ourselves poured out in death. Instead, the athletic images are rather exhilarating. Likewise, the day of judgment, a terrible notion, is transformed into an award celebration. These mysterious transformations of mood are surely the result of faith in a risen Christ. Can death be grievous in view of resurrection? How can judgment be fearful when the judge is one who has died for us?

Notice the sudden interjection in v. 16, "May it not be held against them!" Not only is Paul forgiving those who deserted him, he is waving aside their lapse of loyalty in view of the fine opportunity given him to declare the gospel. Paul seems to believe that every occasion is a moment given by God for evangelism.

The whole passage is filled with confidence, a confidence based on the risen Christ whose ultimate victory is assured (see vv. 8, 18). Yet future hope does not destroy the meaning of life *now*; like a heady athlete, Paul takes delight in the oath, the race, and the fight itself—all in the name of the risen Lord.

GOSPEL: LUKE 18:9–14

The parable of the pharisee and the publican parallels the story of the widow and the corrupt judge. Both are two-character parables, and both are included at the end of a discourse on the coming of the kingdom.

The problem with the parable is that we have heard it preached too often. Ever since Luke built an interpretive framework around the parable, vv. 9 and 14b, the parable has been preached to condemn the self-righteous and appreciate the self-humbling. A radical parable thus has been turned into pious moralism. All we can do is bracket the Lucan interpretation (and the too many sermons) and try to hear the parable all over again in its primal power.

The parable begins and ends with locations: "went up to the temple" and "went down to his house." The locations are more important than we may guess. In the temple, there are those who belong and those who don't belong, the religious in-group and the out-group. Our world of in-church religious values operates much in the same way nowadays; there are "ins," namely, God's believing people, and there are "outs," who are frequently overtly immoral.

The pharisee is definitely in. Though we hear his prayer through Luke's moral judgment as "self-righteous," it was not. Evidently, he was attending one of the daily temple prayer services and, standing in the usual posture of prayer, was contributing his private thanksgiving. His prayer (much like a model prayer quoted in the *Talmud*) is a thanksgiving for God's grace: "There but for the grace of God go I." He gives thanks that by grace alone he has been led into righteousness; he prays, he tithes everything he earns, he fasts twice as often as required. God has given him an upright life, not like crooks, adulterers, or even racketeers (such as the tax collector). Most earnest Christians have thanked God for such virtue as they may possess, and have thought of what they might have been apart from grace. Luke is quite wrong; the pharisee is emphatically not like those who "trusted in themselves." Clearly, he is grateful to God and, in the temple courts, is a model of true piety.

The tax collector was out and for good reason. Tax collectors at the time of Christ were viewed with about as much affection as are Mafia bosses today. They bled their own kin on behalf of the occupying Romans and, in doing so, picked up a tidy profit. Perhaps Jesus' audience would have been appalled by the tax collector's prayer, "God be merciful to me a sinner!" How could God show mercy? For mercy to be given, there would have to be restitution (such as there was with Zacchaeus, Luke 19:8), and how could a systematic tax collector ever repay a whole city? (There is no mention of restitution in the publican's prayer.) The thought of a liturgical confession on the lips of a confirmed racketeer was almost absurd. Tax collectors were hypocrites by definition, particularly when they stood in the temple.

The "veil of the temple is torn" at the conclusion of the parable and, along with it, all our too-sure religious notions of virtue. "Look," says the parable, "this man went down to his house righteous!" (i.e., in the sight of God). All our ins and outs are swept away. Elsewhere Jesus bluntly announces: "The B-girls and the racketeers are entering the kingdom ahead of you" (Matt. 21:31). In the parable of the pharisee and the publican, it happens.

The problem with preaching the parable is that most of us want to find a reason for the reversal in values. Why would God approve a pusher who, in tight jeans and leather jacket, hangs around sleazy places, saying, "I'm no damn good," and bypass an earnest church person who is properly grateful for grace? So, to ease the scandal of the parable, we moralize. The one is self-righteous, egocentric, and stands apart; the other is humble and contritely confesses sins. But the minute we moralize, the parable is lost.

The third character in the parable—God—is barely mentioned. The parable seems to stand amazed by the "wideness in God's mercy," a mercy that constantly overrules our religious definitions by justifying sinners. But the kingdom of God is wider than temple precincts, wider by far than the membership of our churches.

How can we ever restore power to a parable that has been preached too often? How can we cancel out all the moral explanations that have been given?

We can identify with the pharisee's prayer. Most Christians have been startled by unexpected impulses toward charity in themselves. Christians are usually willing to admit that, apart from God's grace, they would be selfish, corrupt, or even carelessly criminal. "There but for the grace of God, go I" is a churchgoer's slogan.

We will have greater difficulty depicting the publican. Who in our culture would be considered quite beyond redemption because of the enormity of their social wrong? Perhaps the organized drug dealer, piously reciting the General Confession, would match the pattern of the parable.

We might even consider adding an additional character to the scene—ourselves. We might picture ourselves sorting out the other two on the basis of our religious judgment; the one seems to be a proud self-righteous man, the other, properly repentant—if only he wasn't such an impossible crook.

We could introduce some shock by realizing that we, the pharisee and ourselves, are left standing behind in the temple while the racketeer heads home "justified." As long as we stay within our churchly definitions, perhaps we can hold on to our righteousness. But there is a strange God—a God who dies for sinners (including pious sinners as well as drug pushers)—with whom we must deal. So maybe we can all stand, say the General Confession, and then sing out the song about a "wideness in God's mercy."

The problem with kingdom parables is that they are so unsettling.

The Twenty-fourth Sunday after Pentecost

Lutheran	Roman Catholic	Episcopal	Common Lectionary
Exod. 34:5–9	Wisd. 11:22—12:1	Isa. 1:10–20	Hag. 2:1–9
2 Thess. 1:1–5, 11–12	2 Thess. 1:11—2:2	2 Thess. 1:1–5 (6–10) 11–12	2 Thess. 1:5–12
Luke 19:1–10	Luke 19:1–10	Luke 19:1–10	Luke 19:1–10

FIRST LESSON: EXODUS 34:5–9

Exodus 34 has been a problem for years. Supposedly, Moses has shattered the original tablets of the law, and here they are reinscribed (v. 1). But in vv. 18–25 we do *not* get a repetition of the original Ten Commandments. Though scholars at the turn of the century tended to regard the chapter as simply another version of the giving of the commandments (Exodus 20), that opinion is no longer argued with confidence. Obviously, the laws that are mentioned are much concerned with ritual observances. Perhaps they have been inserted into what was originally another version (J) of the giving of the decalogue. The puzzle is not easily resolved.

The passage follows a story that began in Exodus 32 when, appalled by out-of-control partying around the golden calf, Moses smashed the tablets of covenant law: "Moses' anger burned hot, and he threw the tablets out of his hands and broke them at the foot of the mountain" (32:19). In chapter 33, Moses prays for his people and God relents; the covenant will be restored. So God orders Moses to climb the mountain alone with new tablets on which the commandments will be reinscribed (34:1–4).

In v. 5, God appears in a cloud descending (see 19:16–18) and, in v. 6, announces the divine name: "The Lord [is] the Lord" (not unlike "I am who I am"). The appearance of God here is portrayed as an answer to Moses who earlier had asked to view God's glory (33:18–23).

Verses 6–7 are a kind of creedal formula that is quoted again and again in the Hebrew Scriptures (see Num. 14:18; Neh. 9:17; Ps. 86:15; etc.). The attributes of God are listed: God is gracious, patient, faithful in love, and forgiving. But God is also just and will not exonerate the stubbornly guilty. Moses responds (vv. 8–9) by bowing down. He intercedes for his people on the basis of God's revealed character; he admits that Israel is a "stiff-necked people," but pleads for mercy—"pardon our iniquity," he says. "Go in the midst of us."

The passage is tricky. Though it is located within a narrative structure

(Exodus 32—34), it is scarcely a story. Instead, the verses are a theophany (v. 5) in which we hear a confession of faith (vv. 6–7) and a response (vv. 8–9).

Perhaps the solution is to set the scene in an introduction, which could depict the cloudy glory of God with little Moses on a mountain. We can then speak of the sheer mystery of God—"The Lord [is] the Lord!" In spite of chummy Christian sermons, God is somehow alien, a holy mystery. How can we little creatures on a tiny planet probe the other-than nature of God? God is who God is!

Of course, the deeper mystery is God's astonishing free covenant-making love for a people (v. 6a). The great God whose glory is like a blinding light, whose mystery is impenetrable, is a self-giver. We were created to be loved. So, according to the Bible, God is a lover who wants to be with free loving children.

We might then turn to admit that we have been unresponsive to God's love; we have been stiff-necked indeed (v. 9a). "We're supposed to love," says the detective in a modern mystery novel; but then adds ruefully, "I flunk. We all flunk." Such is the story of the human race before God.

Obviously, God will not overlook our rebellious sin (v. 7b). For if God is just, then God cannot ignore violations of covenant love. No wonder that, according to the story, Moses shattered the tablets of law. God cares enough for us that God is impatient with our waywardness.

So perhaps all we can do is to pray for mercy (v. 9b). Then maybe we will discover the depth of God's love; in Jesus Christ we know that God forgives (v. 6–7a). God is not an easy touch, but suffers sin. Yet, in love, God does forgive. No wonder that the only way to respond to God is by bowing down in praise (v. 8).

Think of it, the Exodus passage has managed to cram the whole gospel into a handful of verses!

Common Lectionary: Haggai 2:1–9. We are given a marvelous passage from Haggai. To grasp the passage requires an act of imagination.

What to do in a time of "diminished expectations"? Here we are in a rebuilding Jerusalem. While in exile, we dreamed big dreams but now, in the midst of reconstruction, we've had to scale down our dreams. There are, after all, economic realities to be faced. Here we are a month after the foundation for a new temple has been laid, and we are beginning to realize that the new building will not exactly stop traffic. The elderly among us, who still dimly remember Solomon's great temple, are saying the new building is "nothing" compared with what once stood on the spot (v. 3). Gone are the treasures that seemed so full of glory, the silver and gold, the ancient relics. "Diminished expectations!" What can be done in a scaled-down, second-best sort of world?

The prophet Haggai must speak to the people of Jerusalem. What will he have to say as citizens gather at the temple in a festival season (the feast of booths, Lev. 23:33-36)? Three times he says, "Take courage!" and then adds the terse command, "Work!" (v. 4).

Haggai is not merely tossing out a boost for morale. He appeals to the past, recalling God's faithfulness: "I am with you, says the Lord of hosts, according to the promise that I made you when you came out of Egypt." God the liberator, who made covenant with Israel, can be trusted to keep promises.

Then, Haggai dares to scan God's future. "I will shake all nations," God announces, "I will fill this house with splendor." Just as the treasures of the old temple were carried off by plundering nations; so God will cause the nations to return, bringing offerings of silver and gold to fill the temple with richness greater than before (see Isa. 45:14; 60:4-7). Prosperity will surely return to Israel because God keeps promises.

We must not overlook the most perceptive verse in the passage: "My Spirit lives among you!" The presence of God with a people does not depend on religious building programs. The Spirit of God is a promise and a gift. However much we may want to celebrate God's glory with soaring chancels and towers stretching toward the skies, God loves people, obedient faithful people, not lavish places of worship. After all, the whole earth is God's, including mineral rights to silver and gold! Maybe Luther's notion about church buildings should be recalled: Churches, Luther insisted, should be modest like the stable in which Christ was born. What is important is not where we are but that God is with us. "My Spirit lives among you; fear not."

Of course, it is no mistake that Haggai's words end with a vision of the future. Nostalgia is always the enemy of true religion. While we should remember God's goodness in the past, to weep over diminished expectations is a form of unbelief. Surely God is even now working to fulfill the promises; therefore, the future is always full of glory. Haggai looks forward to a day when *all* the earth will honor the Lord. His vision is a better, brighter hope than a reprise of old-time religion (which is popular in America these days). Christian faith, which knows of a risen Christ, always turns eagerly toward the future of God.

SECOND LESSON: 2 THESSALONIANS 1:(1-4) 5-12

What a difficult passage! Verses 1-2 are "stock," the normal form of greeting with which first-century Christian letters began. Likewise, vv. 3-4 are fairly conventional; it was customary to follow initial greetings with an expression of thanks. In a way, vv. 11–12 are not unexpected either, "we always pray for you" or its equivalent shows up in many ancient letters. But in between a conventional greeting and a usual intercession, vv. 5–10 are difficult indeed.

Do not suppose that the author of 2 Thessalonians (perhaps Paul) is dishing out calculated rewards and threats of eternal punishment like some manipulative evangelist ("Oh that will be glory for me"—too bad about you!). Rather, he is preaching to an apocalyptic Christian community that is quite convinced the Lord will return in blazing glory with a troop of angels tagging along (v. 7). Christ will come to usher in a new order, the kingdom of God (v. 5). But the coming of God's new order will involve inevitable judgment; those who believe, who are faithful and loving, will quite naturally fit in (vv. 7a, 10), whereas those who refuse to acknowledge God and have deliberately chosen to live in disobedience will be excluded—perhaps self-excluded (vv. 8–9). The author of 2 Thessalonians is not dealing out rewards and punishments; he is trying to describe (in apocalyptic terms) what will be.

Of course, we must not forget that 2 Thessalonians is evidently addressed to a rather peculiar Christian community. Perhaps they are a millenarian congregation. Rather naively, they seem to have supposed that, with the gift of the Spirit, the new order (aeon) had arrived. But then to their dismay, some members died, nasty conflicts broke out within the congregation, and they encountered social opposition. No wonder the author of 2 Thessalonians praises their constancy in the midst of troubles (v. 4)!

The problem for preachers is that most of our congregations are neither millenarian nor apocalyptic. Notions of the return of the Lord in a 3-D spectacular with angels and fire do not animate our churches. How can we preach the passage faithfully and, at the same time, be honest about an apocalyptic imagery that no longer dances around in our common cultural mind?

The solution may be to take hold of the idea of God's new order (the kingdom of God). If there is to be a new order marked by peace among peoples, distinguished by commonplaces of high courtesy and love, then *inevitably* our present social order and its conventional ways and means must give way. Thus, if God brings about a new way of being together in the world, it will be a judgment on our world as it is now. To tell the truth, it is impossible to pray "Your kingdom come," and then try to hold on tenaciously to life *as is*! No, if God's new world is to be formed, it will mean that our present-tense social order will have to be shaken and, obviously, displaced. Clearly, the Bible—from the prophets to the visionary Book of Revelation—looks forward to the establishing of God's new social order.

Now, the other problem with the passage is what to do with the rigid distinction drawn between those "who have believed" (v. 10) and those "who do not know God" (v. 8). Most clergy are a little nervous when it comes to proclaiming a sharply defined "sheep and goat" theology—we are all fairly ambiguous creatures. In the passage, belief is not intellectual assent, or emotional feeling, or even ritual confession ("I believe in Jesus Christ as my Lord and Savior. Amen."), but rather a way of living involving mutual love (v. 3), steadfastness under fire (v. 4), trusting the testimony of the gospel (v. 10), good resolve, works of faith (v. 11), and the like. We are looking at those who are already seeking to live as citizens of the new order, and those who are going along with the way of the world as if God were not relevant. If we base our lives on the way of the world *now*, a *numero-uno* sort of world, we may be in difficulty in God's new order. Whereas if *now* we are living faithfully in the ways of God's coming new order, then we are already citizens of God's future. "Believing" or "not believing" in the passage are not categories of inner disposition; they are ways of life.

Thus, to preach the passage, we do not need to parade fire and angels before our congregations. Instead, we will have to establish the notion of God's intended new order that, because God is God, shall be—indeed, in a way, already is. Then we can begin to understand "belief" and "unbelief" as ventures of life. No wonder the passage ends in a prayer: May "God make you worthy"; may "the name of our Lord Jesus Christ be glorified among you."

GOSPEL: LUKE 19:1-10

The story of Zacchaeus has been a pulpit favorite for centuries. Details of the story are vivid. We can picture squat, little Zacchaeus straddling the limb of a sycamore tree, trying to spot Jesus passing by. But the passage is not so much concerned with tree climbing as with Jesus Christ who "came to seek and save the lost."

According to the story, Zacchaeus was a "chief tax collector," which may mean that he had a supervisory position or simply that he operated in one of the larger cities, Jericho. He *was* wealthy, says the text emphatically. The name Zacchaeus is ironic. In Hebrew, *zakkai* means "pure" or "innocent," and tax collectors were anything but innocent.

Though we cannot push the detail of Zacchaeus running to climb a tree into a theological statement with regard to conversion (You must want to see Jesus! You must welcome him into your heart!), Luke probably does view his initiative as displaying a degree of religious interest and not mere curiosity. But the story really begins when Jesus happens to look up and spot the tax collector in a tree: "Zacchaeus," he calls, "Hurry up, come down; for *today I must stay at your house.*" Luke is stressing necessity—"I *must* stay," and implying that a stay in Zacchaeus's house is necessary within the saving purposes of God. Given his usual reception around town, Zacchaeus is elated.

The crowd, watching, grumbles, "He has gone to be houseguest of a sinful person." If Jesus were indeed a man of God, they feel, he would not enter the house of Zacchaeus. Instead, he would honor the devout. So, naturally, they grumbled.

The big question in the Zacchaeus story circles around v. 8, which many scholars believe was added to the story by Luke. Certainly it seems to intrude on a natural movement from the crowd's muttering to Jesus' reply. Does the verse imply that for some time Zacchaeus has been virtuous and, here, is simply explaining himself? Or should we read the verse as a spontaneous reaction to Jesus' visit? Do we read the verb in the verse to mean "I continually give . . ." (implying previous action), or as an immediate and future resolve? Given the structure of the passage, it seems better to view the words of Zacchaeus as a response to Jesus' visit. His statement includes the word "Lord," which Luke probably regards as a confession of faith.

Zacchaeus outdoes himself. He gives much more than expected to the poor ("half of my goods"). If he has cheated anyone, he promises to repay quadruple the amount (only an original sum plus one-fifth extra was stipulated in Lev. 6:5 and Num. 5:7). Thus, obviously, Zacchaeus is an extravagant new man!

Now Jesus addresses the crowd. "He also is a son of Abraham," says Jesus, a fairly offensive reply, particularly if v. 8 was not part of the original scenario. What is the basis for the remark? *"Today salvation came to this house!"* is a direct parallel to the words that Jesus spoke to Zacchaeus when the tax collector was up in a tree ("Today I must stay at your house"). God in Jesus Christ has visited a sinner with liberating mercy. So, in God's sight, Zacchaeus is regarded as a child of Abraham.

The final verse of the passage, "For the Son of Man came to seek and to save the lost," is probably an addition, for it gives voice to a favorite theme in Luke's theology.

Though the story of Zacchaeus practically preaches itself, there are some lurking difficulties. In the structural design of the sermon, we will need to rearrange the passage so that v. 8 follows the content of v. 9. We must see Zacchaeus's new resolve as the result of the saving mercy of God. Otherwise, the tax collector's vow of restitution will be regarded as a "work" that qualifies him for salvation.

There is another subtle problem. When Jesus visits sinners, he is often pictured as if he is on a missionary expedition, mingling with rotters not because he likes their company but because, unfortunately, he is supposed to "seek and save the lost." Instead, we must portray a Jesus who genuinely enjoys the company of sinners. Jesus is a lover who takes delight in those he loves. So Jesus *wants* to be with Zacchaeus, despite the fact that he *must*.

At the same time, we must not weaken the accusation against Zacchaeus; he *is* a certifiable sinner! We should not lead congregations to suppose that because Jesus wants to stay with Zacchaeus, the tax collector is not really sinful but deep down has a heart of gold. (So do not make too much of the tree-climbing incident.) No, Zacchaeus was notorious, and with good reason; he was a quisling and an extortioner, and was wealthy because he had systematically victimized the poor. The gospel announces radical good news—*God loves sinners!* We must do nothing to tone down the terms of the gospel. So we must represent the muttering crowd with some sympathy and not write off their reaction as unjustified self-righteousness. The crowd was both right and wrong. Yes, Zacchaeus was indeed a profiteer who grew fat from the poverty of his people. But, no, instead of religious rejection, Jesus did *have* to stay with him. God is a God who seeks and saves the lost.

The Twenty-fifth Sunday after Pentecost

Lutheran	Roman Catholic	Episcopal	Common Lectionary
1 Chron. 29:10–13	2 Macc. 7:1–2, 9–14	Job 19:23–27a	Zech. 7:1–10
2 Thess. 2:13—3:5	2 Thess. 2:16—3:5	2 Thess. 2:13—3:5	2 Thess. 2:13—3:5
Luke 20:27–38	Luke 20:27–38 or Luke 20:27, 34–38	Luke 20:27 (26–33) 34–38	Luke 20:27–38

FIRST LESSON: 1 CHRONICLES 29:10–13

The King David who shows up in Chronicles has been scrubbed clean. Here David is no longer a man who tumbles out of sexual fantasy into bed with Bathsheba, a local beauty who unfortunately happens to be married. He is certainly not pictured as a man with all the savvy of a big-city political boss and twice the ruthlessness. No, David has been cleaned up. He strides through Chronicles with the cinematic bravery of a movie idol and the piety of a saint. The David myth has begun to take shape.

We should not be put off by the idolized David we find in Chronicles. History may be written *about* the past, but it is also written *for* a particular age. The author of Chronicles is not devious; he does not deliberately distort history. No, instead, he selects sources, stressing some and dropping others, for a purpose. While Deuteronomic history was probably written at the time of Josiah's reforms before the exile, trying to recall Israel to God's holy law, Chronicles was written for the frightened, struggling people who returned to Jerusalem after exile and were concerned to begin all over again in a proper way. They were in Jerusalem and, therefore, identified themselves with the Davidic tradition. The chronicler holds up David in such a way as to encourage stable social institutions and, above all, a restoration of temple worship. Remember, history is always written *for* a particular age.

Here is David grown old; he will never live to build the temple. Instead, his stripling son Solomon will have to finish the job. But David has gathered materials—gold, silver, bronze, iron, wood, and building blocks set with precious stones (29:2). In addition, out of his own deep commitment to the temple, David has contributed a chunk of personal wealth—*more* than one hundred tons of gold and two hundred tons of silver! (29:4) The occasion turns into a fund-raiser, as court officials, stirred by Kind David's generosity, contribute even more gold and silver to the building fund, not to mention "precious stones" (29:6–8). No doubt the chronicler has somewhat exaggerated contributions in order to encourage generosity within his own community.

In vv. 10–13, we overhear the beginning of David's prayer of dedication. The prayer is carefully designed: vv. 10b–11 speak of God's greatness; v. 12 mentions God's gifts to all; and v. 13 is an act of thanksgiving and praise. In four short verses we have a capsule theology of worship.

The address is a traditional form of prayer: "Blessed be you, O Yahweh, God of Israel, our father, for ever and ever." Next, David speaks of God's sovereign position—God of greatness, power, and glory, ruler over everything in heaven and on earth. Notice the prayer begins with an address to God, who is known in the tradition of Israel. Then the prayer amplifies God's glory; God is a great God who rules the whole creation.

Abruptly the focus changes: God is the giver of wealth, God is the source of all human strength (v. 12). Think of the great God, the ruler of all creation, giving to *us*! Finally, the prayer breaks into gratitude, praising God's name. The basic nature of Christian worship is thanksgiving. We think of God, the high and holy God, with a kind of primal awe, then recall what God has done for us little creatures, then inevitably give thanks. In Chronicles, David turns into a fine liturgical theologian.

Common Lectionary: Zechariah 7:1–10. Sometimes prophets get the most peculiar questions. On 7 December 518 B.C., a delegation has shown up in Jerusalem with an urgent question for the prophet Zechariah. They seek an oracle of God. For nearly seventy years, as faithful Jews they have fasted to recall the fall of Jerusalem and the destruction of the temple (see 2 Kings 25: 1–2, 8, 25; Jer. 39:1; 41:1–2). Their question is, Now that the temple is being rebuilt, should the fast be continued? What does the prophet have to say on behalf of the Lord?

Eventually, Zechariah will answer that the fast shall be observed, but as a season of "joy and gladness and cheerful feasts" (8:19). To recall the terrible calamity that befell Jerusalem in a new context is to be grateful for deliverance and hopeful toward the future God promises. For someday the whole world will come to the temple to pray, saying to Israel, "God is with you" (8:20–23).

But Zechariah's immediate response is rough. He says that fasting and, by implication, all religious observance, can be empty if people are not doing God's will (vv. 5–6). "When you eat and drink, don't you eat and drink for yourselves?" God observes, implying in the same way that when the people fasted they were fasting for themselves. Repentance is not moaning prayers or harsh self-denials; no, we can be feeding on our own exquisite griefs and self-pity. "Was it for me that you fasted?" God asks point-blank.

Instead, repentance is properly a life-changing moral purpose. True religion is always ethical. So Zechariah is quite explicit: "Thus says the Lord of hosts, Render true judgments, show kindness and mercy.... Do not oppress the widow, the orphan, the foreigner, the poor...." (vv. 8–10; see Jer. 7:5–6; 22:3). The delegation that came to Zechariah with a question about religious observance has ended up being questioned by a moral God!

American Protestant denominations can worry much over trivia: What are the proper stoles to wear during the seasons of the Church Year? Can we receive communion in the hand or not? Shall we relocate our denominational headquarters in Louisville or Kansas City? Meanwhile the homeless huddle in our streets, a defense budget escalates out of control, and weapons are traded to Iran to pay for death squads (not

The Twenty-fifth Sunday after Pentecost

"freedom fighters") in Central America. A sermon on Zechariah will almost write itself!

The final answer given in 8:18–22 is worth examining, even though it is not included in the lection. In light of the resurrection and the surprising signs of new life among us, we celebrate the death of Christ gratefully. We even hoist high crosses in our churches. Nevertheless, the harshness of the cross must not be forgotten lest our gratitude turn into mindless hoopla. Israel had been delivered from exile, yes, but if Israel should forget the disobedience that led to exile, they would never grasp the full mercy of their return to Jerusalem. So, though they celebrate old feasts with new gratitude, they must still continue to remember the terrible fall of the city.

Furthermore, they are to look toward God's future—as do Christians. We can easily forget that our deliverance is a part of God's eternal purpose. To say Christ died for *us* may be a fine personal statement of faith, but it can slip into nasty religious exclusivism. We must never forget that the death of Christ is connected with God's ultimate purpose, namely, the redemption and reconciliation of the world. Christian faith also looks toward a day when "every knee should bow . . . and every tongue confess that Jesus Christ is Lord, to the glory of God."

Between the cross and the glory we are called to repent and to obey. We can get by quite nicely without liturgical etiquette, but we cannot live without ethical concern to do justly and love mercy in the sight of a holy God. Zechariah was remarkably specific, and we must be as concrete. To do justly and love mercy involves caring for street people, providing low-cost housing, reducing our military budget, and increasing provision for the poor of our land.

How else can we devoutly respond to Jesus the Christ?

SECOND LESSON: 2 THESSALONIANS 2:13—3:5

The passage from 2 Thessalonians is peculiar. The start of 2:13 duplicates 1:3, just as, in 1 Thessalonians, 2:13 echoes 1:2, leading some scholars to wonder if 2 Thessalonians is not a clever imitation of the first letter. Other scholars ask why we have two "thanksgiving/prayer" sections in the letter, supposing that vv. 13–17 are from some other letter and have been pasted into 2 Thessalonians. The queries cannot be resolved and for preaching are not crucial. As the passage stands, we have a "thanksgiving" (vv. 13–15) followed by two "prayer" sections (2:16–17; 3:1–5), both of which sound as if they might be conclusions. Any of these units can be preached.

Verse 13b may be paraphrased, " . . . you, who have been loved by

Christ, were chosen by God from the beginning to be saved, by faith in the Truth and the sanctifying of the Spirit." There is debate over the phrase "*from* the beginning," and some translators render it "*as* the first to be saved." But, all in all, "from the beginning" is preferable. The author is saying that salvation is God's eternal purpose; God has loved us from the beginning and thus has determined to set us free to share in the glory of Christ Jesus (14b).

How has God carried out the saving purpose? By reaching out to us through the preaching of the gospel (14). So we must stand firm in the gospel "tradition," which we have heard by word of mouth or read in letters. Notice that God's eternal purpose is to be carried out by such seemingly mundane activities as speaking and writing (15).

No wonder that, suddenly, thanksgiving turns into prayer (vv. 6–17): May Jesus Christ and God strengthen faith and establish all we do or say! (Notice the parallel between "do and say" and the earlier reference to letters and words.) The prayer that follows in 3:1–5 echoes many of these same concerns, although it reaches clear beyond us with a concern for the continued evangelical mission of the church (3:1).

In preaching the passage do we need to speak at length of Paul and Timothy? No, the passage addresses us today. Are we not a being-saved people? And have we not been gripped by hearing and reading the story of God-with-us in Jesus Christ?

After an introduction, the movement of a sermon can be traced. (1) Here we are in church. In spite of our brokenness, we are dimly aware that our lives are being shaped in a new way. However worldly we may be, we do have surprising impulses toward charity, concern for our neighbors, and mutual acceptance. Oh, we must not be self-righteous, but we can be surprised by the hidden working of grace in our lives. (2) Well, maybe it's because we have heard the gospel. Way back in childhood, did we not hear stories of Jesus? Did we not sing our little songs— "Jesus loves me this I know!" So maybe the words of the gospel have formed us more deeply than we know—the stories, the Bible study, the sermons in church on Sunday. And not just words—we have lived together sharing a Spirit of love. People care for us and we for them. Gradually, by Word and Spirit, our lives are being changed. (3) Guess what? God has been at work. From the beginning God made us. And from the beginning God has wanted to live in love with a people. Through the long centuries God has been drawing us toward communion. Do we not see such love in Jesus Christ? Here is a God dying for us sinful people, yet risen to come to us, deliver us, and bring us to communion! (4) But see how God works! God doesn't dazzle us into faith, or arm-twist our convictions. No, God comes to us through words.

Remember the prophets who, though strident, called us to obedience. Think of the early apostles scurrying around the ancient world talking news of God. Or how about the frontier horseback preachers plodding across our wild land with the word of God? All along, God has been working with words; the childhood Bible stories, the study circles, the sermons we still hear. (5) So let us stand in the faith God has given us. Let us be together in the Spirit, and by our words strengthen each other in faith. Let us be a new kind of people faithful to God and gleeful in charity. From the beginning God has wanted us to be a people in communion. Together, let us fulfill God's purpose for us. (6) But, look out, we almost forgot. God's purpose is larger than we know; God is seeking a world. We are not called to wallow in our own salvation, but to reach out to others, to all the other people God calls. So we must share the Spirit of love we have been given and, above all, speak. For, remember, rather modestly, God chooses to use words for the liberation of the world; please note, *our* words.

We have not talked about verses from the passage, or mentioned Paul and Timothy. Instead, we have simply articulated the pattern of gospel from the passage for congregations today.

GOSPEL: LUKE 20:27–38

Here is a controversy. The controversy form in Scripture normally involves a question, a counterquestion, and then an epigrammatic pronouncement. Here, we have a question (vv. 28–33) and we have a pronouncement (v. 38), but the usual crisp pattern of question/counterquestion has been somewhat disrupted, leading a few scholars to suppose that the passage involves a combination of sources. Trick questions were often posed by sadducees, who on the basis of the Torah denied resurrection in order to trap pharisees, who looked for a resurrection of the righteous (Dan. 12:2–3). But here we may be dealing with a genuine concern of early Jewish-Christian communities: What will resurrection mean for us and those we love?

The question posed in the passage has to do with so-called levirate marriage. If a woman was left childless by the early death of a husband, it was the duty of her brother-in-law to take her as a wife and produce children so as to continue his dead brother's line (see Gen. 38:8; Deut. 25:5–10). Though levirate marriage was probably not practiced at the time of Christ, the custom (multiplied by seven!) did provide a thorny theoretical question: "In the resurrection, therefore, whose wife will the woman be?" Jesus answers by insisting that the resurrection implies a whole new order. In this present world, we have to procreate to continue life, but in the new age there will be no such need because "they cannot die anymore" (v. 36).

Then, Jesus adds another argument, citing words from the Torah (Exod. 3:6). When God spoke to Moses from the burning bush, God proclaimed, "I am . . . the God of Abraham, the God of Isaac, and the God of Jacob." Since, at the time, the patriarchs were dead, somehow they must still "live to God" because God "is not a God of the dead but of the living" (v. 38).

Picky arguments between sadducees and pharisees no longer agitate congregations today. Instead, twentieth-century Christians may have different, more basic questions: How can we believe in resurrection? and, If we do believe in resurrection what happens to our human relationships? The theology of the passage—God is a God of life, not death, who calls us to live in a new order—can still address us.

We must not forget that the controversy in Luke was redesigned for a Christian community that confessed a risen Christ. So they were hearing words of a risen Christ testifying to a God of the living, and promising a new order larger than the sometimes narrow confines of family obligation. Marriage ties may be pledged "'til death do us part," but they cannot determine the sweet, much wider shape of a risen family of God. The communion we have with one another may be a rehearsal for the communion of saints.

Just lately there seems to be a growing interest in life after death. Perhaps we are beginning to sense that when it comes to dying, therapy is not enough! We need to know. For death, even when covered up by cosmetics and floral sprays, is still fearfully final. A college student came rushing into a chaplain's office, eyes bulging, cold sweat on his forehead, stammering, "I've just realized someday I'm going to die!" That same someday faces us all; the mortality rate still runs 100 percent!

What does Jesus say? "God is a God of the living!" Remembering the good news of Easter Day, his words are full of hope. No, not hope in our own survival. We are not immortal; no secret part of us will survive death. But, nevertheless, we hope in Christ Jesus, whom God raised up. Christ is risen and we look to be with him, who has lived for us and died for us in love. So we trust God's love.

Of course, resurrection is no mere extension of here and now; the key word is *new*. If life after death is only an extension of things as they are, it's a terrible prospect. Do we want to live on and on in our brokenness? "You can't take it with you" is a cheering slogan. We must leave behind not only cash but our broken selves. *New* is the word. Resurrection is news of a whole new order of life in the glory of God.

Suddenly the questions come tumbling out! What identity will we have? And what about those we love? Will a new order sweep away all that is good and graceful in our lives? Do we wake, risen, like newborn infants with memory obliterated? Somehow as we live with others we love, they become built-in to who we are. Are even our loves discarded? Think it out; we will be *together* in the Lord, but in a new way. Christian faith doesn't promise personal survival. No, it speaks of the whole body of Christ raised up. Family ties are not an ultimate. Sometimes family ties can even prevent us from reaching out to the wider family of God—all our brothers and sisters, mothers and fathers, and children on earth. No wonder, as Christians, we celebrate the wonderful hope of a Communion of Saints.

So, get ready, get set, right now let us begin to enlarge our loves until we embrace all God's children—a little resurrection practice in advance!

The Twenty-sixth Sunday after Pentecost

Lutheran	Roman Catholic	Episcopal	Common Lectionary
Mal. 4:1–2a	Mal. 4:1–2a	Mal. 3:13—4:2a, 5–6	Mal. 4:1–6
2 Thess. 3:6–13	2 Thess. 3:7–12	2 Thess. 3:6–13	2 Thess. 3:6–13
Luke 21:5–19	Luke 21:5–19	Luke 21:5–19	Luke 21:5–19

FIRST LESSON: MALACHI 4:1–6

The formidable passage that concludes Malachi needs to be read in the context of chapter 3, vv. 14–18. God looks over the world. Some people have wandered away into calculated unbelief, asking, in effect, "What do we get out of being religious? Look at unbelievers, they're successful. They aren't burdened by conscience; they are happy!" (3:13–15). But others are faithful; they discuss the Lord's will together. I have a record of them, God notes, and in the day of judgment they will be spared (3:16–18).

Then, Malachi launches a vivid description of the day of judgment. In 4:1, the day is likened to a furnace in which the arrogant will be reduced to stubble. But God will shine like a morning sun on those who revere God, (4:2). The image, found only here in the Hebrew Scriptures, may draw on the notion of a winged sun-god pictured in Egyptian and

Mesopotamian art. More likely, the verse may have been influenced by Zoroastrian religion, which also spoke of a "sun of righteousness" and a fiery consummation. Of course, there are verses in the Psalms that suggest that the light of God will rise on the righteous or that the faithful will see God's help in the morning. Malachi pictures the faithful being as frisky as a prancing calf, yet trampling the burnt-over wicked under foot. Possibly the Book of Malachi originally ended with this odd but fearful image.

We get two appendices, v. 4 and vv. 5–6, which were probably tacked on by later editors. In the Septuagint, v. 4 is located after vv. 5–6 so that the collection of the twelve prophets would not end with the words of v. 6b, "lest I come and smite the land with a curse." For the same reason, in Jewish liturgy it was customary in reading the passage to repeat v. 5 as a final conclusion.

Verse 4 concludes the book by adding an injunction to remember (i.e., obey) the "law of my servant Moses," thus connecting the words of the prophets with the Torah. Verse 5 is a still later conclusion, possibly reflecting a rise of apocalyptic thinking that displayed lively interest in Elijah (e.g., Ecclus. 48:1–11, which also includes mention of a reconciliation of fathers and sons). The belief that there would be a return of Elijah before the day of judgment seems to have been based on the tradition in 2 Kings 2:1–12 in which Elijah is caught up into heaven. (The return of Elijah shows up in the Gospel of Mark, 6:15; 15:35.) Here the idea is that Elijah, coming before the judgment, could still convert *all* Israel (v. 6a). Of course, Christians have viewed Jesus Christ as the fulfillment of the conclusion to Malachi (Luke 1:17).

How are we to preach a passage that, at least in 3:13—4:3, rigidly divides the human race into the faithful and the "arrogant"? In our churches, there is already quite enough triumphalist hand-rubbing over the fate of the wicked without any more pulpit encouragement! Clearly, we must read the passage not only in the light of v. 6, where there is hope for all the children of Israel, but also in view of the Christian Scriptures.

Yet we cannot bypass the moral earnestness of Malachi. The "arrogant" are arrogant not because they question the good of being righteous (Job and other devout questioners seem to have been good friends of God), but because they are living as practical atheists; they ignore the precepts of God and trample neighbors. They embody "bad faith." Clearly God cannot approve violations of covenant responsibility by casual, if calculating, people. The faithful, by contrast, are not concerned for a religious payoff; they are curious about the things of God and are seeking to learn (and do) God's will. Thus, they live toward God. And God, in turn, is pleased with them.

The added endings are, in sequence, quite wonderful. In faith, we are able to link together Moses and Elijah and their fulfillment in Jesus Christ, who gives the teaching of God and recalls us to faithfulness, so that all God's children may be reconciled. Surely the last words of the Hebrew Scriptures are on tiptoe to see the coming of the Lord Christ.

In preaching the passage, we may have to reach back into the previous chapter of Malachi so as to picture our "arrogant" world. (1) Chasing success and happiness, our world ignores the law of God. (2) God will not tolerate such casual disdain, which leads to self-destruction. (3) So we are called to get together and by studying to seek God's will for us. (4) What do we end up with? A self-destructive world except for a righteous remnant in the light of God's approval? (5) No. God has sent Jesus Christ, crucified and risen, so that we may still turn—all of us together—to embrace God's will and be reconciled.

SECOND LESSON: 2 THESSALONIANS 3:6–13

Unfortunately, the passage from 2 Thessalonians has often been aimed as a weapon against the indigent or cited as justification for a capitalist work ethic. But, if anything, it chastises the idle rich who could afford to be religious dilettantes while waiting for the Parousia.

The problem is not new. In 1 Thessalonians, Paul drops in the phrase "admonish the idle" (5:14). Evidently, there has been further news from Thessalonica about the same free-loading Christians who, unoccupied, have time to be "busybodies" (v. 11). Obviously, these idlers were affluent; slaves could scarcely stop working. The author of the letter, "in the name of the Lord," urges people in the congregation to stay away from these idle rich (v. 6). He is not advising an excommunication but is simply suggesting that the rest of the congregation should not join them in idleness and foolish chatter.

Paul points to himself. While he was in Thessalonica as a missionary, he could have properly claimed their support (v. 9). Instead, he earned his own keep rather than be a burden on the congregation (v. 8). To support his argument, he quotes what was evidently a well-known proverb: "If anyone will not work, let him not eat." Then he drops in a final word: "Do not be weary in well-doing," which in the context of the discussion may mean that the congregation is not to put off dealing with the idlers.

Why were there Christians who were unoccupied? Did they suppose that Christian freedom meant that they were to be free from the burden of work? Were they too pious to work, busy at "spirituality"? Or had they simply stopped working while they waited for the coming of the Lord? The fact that Paul says pointedly that they did not *learn* their idleness from him (v. 6b) seems to indicate that their position was based on some sort of religious conviction. Whatever the attitude, we can assume that there was an underlying assumption, namely, that religious thinking is of a higher, more "spiritual" order than mere physical activity.

Is there some general theological truth tucked into the passage? Perhaps. Certainly, 2 Thessalonians believes that members of Christian community have mutual obligations. Therefore, we must work to support one another and to contribute to the community's charitable concerns. If we can help ourselves, we should not be a drain on community resources. Christian faith is not a private inwardness or a personal predilection, but a common shared purpose in Christ Jesus.

Does the author say anything about the dignity of work? No, he neither denigrates work as a penalty of the Fall (Gen. 3:19) nor celebrates it as a way of giving God glory. Though many Greeks regarded physical work as demeaning, the author seems to see value in hard work, but *not* in and of itself; work is a way of supporting Christian community in its evangelical purpose.

Let us be candid. Second Thessalonians 3:6–13 is not a passage for Labor Day sermons. Instead, it calls us to Christian community in which each of us contributes to the good of all. The passage also may warn us against any peculiar form of Christian "spirituality" that cadges on the sweat of others.

A sermon on this passage could begin by describing the idlers as religious people, deeply committed to a "spiritual" life. They live aloof from the push and shove of every day, dedicated to their own religious enlightenment. Endlessly they chatter together of the things of God. Above all, they think of themselves as somehow living a higher life apart from the mundane, all-too-physical world that others inhabit.

Well, one does wonder what they thought of Jesus Christ, born in a cow stall, hung on a cross. There is something fiercely physical about his passion: A crown of thorns was crushed on his head, and nails knocked into his limbs. He sweat under the weight of his cross. And, as he died, he bawled for a drink: "I thirst," he cried. And yet, do we not speak of him with a hush, confessing, "Here is God-with-us"?

There is no way we can live for others except bodily. Self-sacrifice for others is always a bodily act done in bodily places. Whether we are making love or serving in a soup kitchen or waiting beside a hospital bed, we are always physically involved. On the cross, Jesus did not whirl his glazed eyes toward heaven and announce, "I feel a spiritual love for you all." No, he died.

What's more, if we want to live for God we must do so bodily. Yes, we should give our brains to search the mystery, to learn all that we can of God's holy will. But we must not forget that God gave us flesh and bone, our bodies, so that in turn we might give ourselves to a Godly life, physically. We do not serve God in lone, lofty spiritual climates. No, our problem is to find out how to serve God while living in families, doing jobs, eating and sleeping and, yes, even dying.

Now do you see why we are here together in church? Here we practice the new life. In worship, we bow and stand and sing in fine, physical ways. And we serve one another, reaching out with our hands and words and our work. Here we practice our life together in the Spirit; and it is a truly physical life for one another and for God.

GOSPEL: LUKE 21:5-19

Though Luke draws heavily on the "little apocalypse" in Mark 13, he also gathers in themes previously discussed (a call to fearless testimony, 12:1-12, 35-59; dismay over Jerusalem, 13:34-35; 19:41-48; and the coming of the Son of man, 17:20-37) and projects events that in fact will take place in Acts. The lectionary has selected the first part of a two-part discourse (vv. 5-19; 20-36), each part of which concludes with a call to faithful discipleship.

The passage is prompted by someone speaking of "noble stones" in the temple. (The second temple was a more modest edifice than the temple Solomon completed. But during the time of Herod a remodeling program was initiated to enlarge and enhance the building. The refurbishing of the temple continued during Jesus' lifetime and almost up to the time of its destruction.) In reply, Jesus speaks a prophetic oracle, not unlike Mic. 3:11-12 or Jer. 22:5: "The days will come when there shall not be left here one stone upon another." Then people asked a natural question, "When?" And Jesus, in answer, launches an apocalyptic address.

What will be the signs of the end? First, there will be false prophets who speak in his name (vv. 8-9); then, there will be political upheavals (v. 10, also 20-24); then, cosmic disturbances (v. 11, also 25-26); and finally, the coming of the Son of man (v. 27). Please notice that, though Luke may mention dire happenings, he nevertheless assumes Christians should rejoice (v. 28) because the new order is arriving. Apocalyptic language is transformed from threat to joy by Christian hope.

Meanwhile, before the signs of the end, Christians will have it rough (v. 12). Luke predicts what Acts will tell; Christians will be harassed by Jewish leaders (Acts 4—5, 12, 16, 18, 21) and hauled before kings and governors (Acts 24—26). Such persecution will call for testimony (v. 13).

Don't try to figure out what you will say ahead of time, Jesus advises. "I will give you a mouth and wisdom" (v. 15, perhaps recalling Exod. 4:15). Then Jesus predicts that Christians will be betrayed by family and friends. "You will be hated for my sake," he says. But then, quoting a proverbial phrase, he adds, "Not a hair of your head will perish." Instead, Christian endurance will gain life ("Whoever will lose life, will gain it").

The passage is an odd mix of prophecy, apocalyptic prediction, and exhortation. The problem for preachers is that twentieth-century Americans do not have a Jewish apocalyptic mindset. (Certainly we do not wish to encourage tent-meeting timetables for the end of the world!) Yet the passage *is* cosmic, and cannot be turned into a personalism such as someday each of our personal worlds will end in death, meanwhile let's be good Christians. Luke pictures a time of chaos and persecution; he is not addressing personal religion. The bald embarrassment is that at least in America nobody seems to be persecuting us, perhaps because our version of Christian faith has been culturally accommodative. So how on earth can we preach the passage here and now?

There may be a clue in the structural design of the passage. Notice that the exchange at the start of the passage involves admiration by an onlooker in the temple, prompting a prophetic oracle from Jesus announcing the destruction of the edifice. The temple was surely the central symbol of Jewish national and religious identity. Jesus is clearly saying that the religious institutions of Israel have become moribund; they no longer give life. But there is more to the oracle than condemnation. Jesus was speaking with an eye toward a new aeon in which there would be a new kind of temple, as well as a whole new social order, namely, the kingdom. At a time when America seems to be trying to hold on to itself, its power, its institutions, even its denominationalism, the gospel of God's new order is still unwelcome. To proclaim the new order of God is, at the same time, to announce the demise of *our* social world—including our economic systems, political theories, and the forms of our religious institutions. The crisis underlying Luke's strange passage is a crisis of the coming of God's new order as a judgment on our social orders.

So a sermon might be designed by beginning with Jesus' unwelcome prophecy—"Not one stone shall be left on another!" In our land, the words are still unwelcome. Are we not filled with admiration for all that we have accomplished: our towering cities, our military power, our democracy, and, above all, the sense of God within our public life? Look at our churches; there are steeples topping every town in the land. Yet, the word of Christ is sharp: "Not one stone shall be left on another."

Of course, when you think about it, his words are not unexpected. With Christ, do we not believe in a coming new age of God? We pray each day, "Your kingdom come!" Well, if God's kingdom comes, what about the world we live in? Our systems are scarcely perfect. Is there full justice in our courts? Are there not poor in the land? And what about our competing churches—can anyone claim that denominational rivalry is what God intends? When Christian faith announces the coming of God's new order, it also says by implication that our way of life will be past tense!

Is it any wonder, then, that the gospel is not exactly popular? If we have built our prosperity into "things as they are," can we welcome a new kind of world? No. A church that truly preaches the kingdom of God will be persecuted. Oh, it may not be as bad for us as the Bible supposes—persecuted in churches, hauled into court, betrayed by friends. Nevertheless, if we tell people of God's new order in Christ Jesus, we can expect to arouse hostility.

For heaven's sake, don't worry! Think of being crowded "up against the wall" so that we have to testify to our faith. Perhaps peace protesters these days have a chance to say what they believe, or possibly Christians who are caught up in the Sanctuary movement. But, if we declare the gospel boldly, we can sense that our time will come. What will we say? Don't worry, says Jesus, I will give you words to say. Maybe this is happening to us already, as we study the Bible together and listen to sermons and sing our faith in church. We are being given words to say by the Lord Jesus Christ. We need not worry.

Well, at least our lives would be exciting! To live for Christ boldly would be l-i-f-e spelled out in bright letters, life indeed. Remember Martin Luther King, Jr., sitting in a Birmingham jail, realizing that although persecuted he was somehow more alive than ever before. Be honest; our little churchiness can be tedious. But in the gospel, affairs can be soul-sized. All it takes is courage to live for God's new social order, saying and praying, "Your kingdom come."

The passage is exceedingly difficult. We are not proposing a particular sermon, but merely suggesting one peculiar way of trying to solve the problems posed by Luke's call to discipleship.

Christ the King
The Last Sunday after Pentecost

Lutheran	Roman Catholic	Episcopal	Common Lectionary
Jer. 23:2-6	2 Sam. 5:1-3	Jer. 23:1-5	2 Sam. 5:1-5
Col. 1:13-20	Col. 1:12-20	Col. 1:11-20	Col. 1:11-20
Luke 23:25-43	Luke 23:35-43	Luke 23:35-43 or Luke 19:29-38	John 12:9-19

FIRST LESSON: JEREMIAH 23:2-6

The passage is composed of two different oracles, vv. 1-4 and vv. 5-6. The first is a "Woe" Oracle against irresponsible kings ("shepherds") of Israel, while the second promises the coming of a rightful descendant of David to rule the land.

Verses 1-4 are a tough oracle against leaders who have misled the people so that, as a result, the people have been scattered. The notion of the scattering of the sheep has led many scholars to suppose that the oracle was not from Jeremiah, but was added after the exile. However, if the phrase "out of all the countries where I have driven them" (v. 3) is a later addition, then the rest of the oracle is very much in the style of Jeremiah. There is a play on words in v. 2: "You . . . have not *tended* them; I am going to *tend* to you . . ." There is another repetition worth noticing: the phrase "you for your part have scattered my sheep" (v. 2b) is matched by the start of v. 3, "I for my part will gather . . ." The phrase in v. 3, "be fruitful and multiply," is an allusion to God's covenant command to Abraham and Jacob. Finally, in v. 4, God promises to secure proper shepherds to watch over what is left of the flock.

The second oracle (vv. 5-6) is duplicated in Jer. 33:15-16. Perhaps it follows vv. 1-4 because in both cases we have the phrase "I will appoint" (vv. 4, 5), a repetition that is obscured in the RSV translation. An oracle announcing a royal savior (such as Isa. 11:1-9) is unusual in Jeremiah. In v. 6, the name of the new king in Hebrew seems to be a reversal of Zedekiah's name, perhaps to indicate that the promised ruler will reverse Zedekiah's foolish policies. The name is translated "the Lord is our righteousness." The image of the "branch" in v. 5 (similar to Isa. 11:1) is picked up in Zech. 3:8 where it is used as a messianic title. Obviously, the image has been significant in the Jewish messianic tradition and in Christian theology.

The two oracles can be preached in a single sermon by allowing the prediction of a royal savior to inform the promise of good shepherds for the people.

Certainly most Americans understand the phrase "crisis in leadership"; we are living in the midst of such a crisis. Every four years we push into voting booths hoping to elect leaders for the land. But of late we have been sadly disillusioned. How often are public mandates followed by indictments, investigations, or worse? As for religious leadership, is it much better? You do wonder of late if PTL does not stand for "Pass the Lucre"! Talk about shepherds who fail to care for the people! We can document the fact.

What is the result? The result is a divided America. We flag-wave our patriotism but scuttle our own long-held values. We talk of being peace lovers, but we have become the number-one exporters of death. We revere our image as a welcome mat for the impoverished immigrant, but end up holding "sanctuary" trials. Somehow or other we have allowed ourselves to be misled.

Do not suppose that God is unconcerned! "Woe to you leaders who destroy morality and divide the land!" All leadership is ultimately under the leadership of God. So if national goals aim in a different direction from God's purpose, will God bend? No; if leadership misleads, God will lead leaders into futility.

Fear not! The promise speaks to us. Fear not, and don't be discouraged! God cares enough for the human world to raise up new leadership. There will be honorable leaders and good teachers, worthy preachers and sensitive managers; so God has promised. For ultimately our land is not ours—God alone is sovereign over the heavens and the earth. We may vote, but God appoints. God's promises will be kept.

Well, according to the gospel, God's promise has been kept; Jesus Christ has come among us. He has instructed our wills, united us in Spirit, and shown us God's own way and truth and life. Yes, the cross is witness to our open revolt; all together, leaders and people, we rejected God's rule. But, nevertheless, Christ is raised up, and God's promise is fulfilled. The human world *has* a leader, God's leadership, in Jesus Christ the Lord.

So maybe now we are called to follow the leader! "At the right hand of God," the creed declares, acknowledging the rule of Jesus Christ. How to follow Jesus Christ? We can work for peace—"Blessed are the peace makers." We can give charitably to neighbors—"Blessed are the poor." And surely we can stand up for justice—"Blessed are those who hunger for righteousness." The real "crisis of leadership" is a crisis of faith. Now we can choose to follow God's own appointed leader, Jesus Christ the Lord.

Common Lectionary: 2 Samuel 5:1-5. This alternative passage is also concerned with kingship; it tells of David being chosen king of Israel. The oldest record of David's rise to power is possibly v. 3, which, significantly, depicts leadership as a "covenant." Verses 1-2 are probably a Deuteronomic addition and certainly the chronological information in vv. 4-5 has also been appended. Though the passage is brief it is important.

Verses 1-2 tell of *all* the people coming together to select David. They say, "We are your own flesh and bone," and they admit that, even while Saul was king, David was their effective leader. They believe that God has spoken, saying, "You shall be shepherd of my people Israel." Whatever the political process, Israel believes that in their elections God is also electing.

Verse 3 tells a somewhat different story. Here representative elders of the tribes gather at Hebron; David makes covenant with them (a mutual agreement) and is subsequently anointed king. Anointing was understood as a divine recognition. David was thus "the Lord's anointed."

Verses 4-5 present a somewhat idealized chronology. David's seventy-year life span is a perfect age. The other times cited may be more accurate. Notice that David is king over "Israel and Judah," a yoked kingdom which of course eventually split.

The passage is not without some theological depth. A ruler's right to rule is based on covenant; though there may be free choosing involved, nevertheless there are mutual responsibilities. Thus, political covenants are meant to mirror God's covenant with people. David is of the people, "bone and flesh," yet by popular consent is to rule over people.

The crucial notion that lies hidden in the passage is of God's choice. Kings in Israel were a compromise, because the true king of Israel was obviously Yahweh. Therefore, kingship was always conducted under the acknowledged kingship of God. While people may select, God ultimately elects and anoints.

Through the centuries, Christians have affirmed the notion that Jesus *Christ* ("anointed"), a descendant of David, is God's appointed ruler of the human world. Though Jesus was "bone and flesh" with us, his loving rule is an expression of God's covenant. Though God has raised up Christ, like the ancient people of Israel we are to acknowledge his rule by faith and true obedience.

The passage is brief and so may seem difficult to shape into a sermon. But it does address our world: What kind of leader do we seek? Certainly, whoever leads us must be from among us, bone and flesh. Some high cloudy alien will not do. We seek someone who can understand all that it means to be human, our fears, our fallibilities, our longings.

The Last Sunday after Pentecost

And yet, God save us from a leader who is merely human! We will need someone who, living among us, is still somehow in touch with God's will. A man in an airport restaurant, bleakly reading newspaper headlines, slapped his hand down on the paper and exclaimed, "Anyone who'd straighten out the mess we're in, we'll elect 'em God!" Somehow, we do need a God-sized leader.

No wonder we bow down before Jesus Christ. He was no demagogue, feeding on his own sense of power. He called himself a servant, he died helpless as all human beings die. And yet, surely he is of God. "Not my will, but yours be done!" he cried. He gives mercy and, at the same time, judgment. No wonder we sing his praise: "King of Kings, Lord of Lords."

God has raised him up to be our Lord, but he waits our free choosing. After all, does he not embody God's covenant: "I will be your God and you will be my people." Power does not command allegiance; love does. Christ's rule is freedom.

So let us choose the Leader that God has chosen.

SECOND LESSON: COLOSSIANS 1:12–20

Whoever wrote Colossians was fond of quoting. The standard letter began with a greeting, a thanksgiving, and a prayer. Here we have the customary "prayer section" of a letter (vv. 9–11) leading into an expression of joyful gratitude (vv. 12–14), followed by the quotation of a two-stanza hymn (vv. 15–20). Probably the hymn was familiar to the congregation in Colossae.

The language in vv. 12–14 is peculiar. Probably the author is drawing on some sort of liturgical material, perhaps from a baptismal service. We are called to give thanks to God, the parent, who has qualified us to share in "the inheritance of the saints in light" (v. 12). "Inheritance" is a term connected with the tradition of promised land, but which in time became an image of all that God holds in store for faithful believers. While some scholars suppose that the phrase "saints in light" refers to angels, it probably means Christians who are living in God's light. Such a reading is supported by the next verse (v. 13), which says that we have been transferred from "the dominion of darkness" to the kingdom of God's well-loved Son. The metaphors are spatial; we have been shifted from one sphere of influence to another—from a realm of darkness into the light of Christ's saving love. Our liberation from darkness has been by means of a release from our sins (v. 14). Though these verses are difficult to unpack, basically they celebrate God's liberation in our lives.

Then, the author of Colossians lines out a two-stanza hymn celebrating creation and redemption. Each stanza begins with an affirmation of

Christ: "He is the image of the invisible God, the first-born of all creation" (v. 15) and "He is the beginning, the first-born of the dead" (v. 18b). And each stanza develops with the same secondary phrase, "for in him . . ." It is likely, however, that the author has added phrases to the original stanzas, possibly "whether thrones or dominions or principalities or authorities" (v. 16b), and almost certainly "the church" (v. 18a) and "by the blood of the cross" (v. 20b).

What kind of song is being quoted? Perhaps we are hearing a wisdom hymn not unfamiliar in Hellenistic Judaism and often addressed to Sophia, the personification of God's wisdom (Wisd. Sol. 7:25—8:21). A similar hymn may underlie the prologue in the Gospel of John.

The first stanza lines out a high Christology. Christ is "first-born," meaning *preeminent* (not first of a sequence). He is the preexistent "image of God," through whom and for whom the whole creation was created. (Much the same notion is expressed in a hymn to Wisdom found in Prov. 8:22–31.) So "image" is not a reference to Gen. 1:27, but is rather a Greek understanding; God is "mirrored" in Christ, and the creation in turn embodies the mirroring of God-in-Christ. Notice that the "principalities and powers" are also created and thus subservient to Christ.

The second stanza celebrates Christ as the Lord of the new creation, "first-born from the dead." Christ, filled with the "fullness of God" (the overflow of God's own goodness and harmony), acts to reconcile all things, thus restoring harmony and goodness to the universe. Note the repetition of "earth and heaven" (vv. 16a; 20), which indicates that reconciliation fulfills the true purpose of creation.

Can you see what the additions to the hymn do? Here we have a high, soaring hymn of praise, singing the purposes of God-in-Christ for the universe—and what has been tacked on? Why, mention of "the church" (v. 18b) and of "the blood of his cross" (v. 20b)—a ghastly execution and a gaggle of confused congregations! Here a high Christology drops into the small-time specifics of our human history.

The idea of a preexistent Christ through whom the world was created may seem an elaborate myth that somehow distorts the simple gospel of Jesus. Not so; there is a crucial theological issue at stake. If we do not regard Christ as the purpose of creation, he becomes no more than an emergency measure taken by a desperate God to deal with stubborn human sinfulness. Our sins then become the whole reason for Jesus Christ. But if all along God has intended communion with humanity (i.e., Jesus Christ), then Christ is not only our Savior but the image of our true humanity before God.

How can we preach a complex passage full of quotes? We can build a theological structure. Some years ago a church, celebrating its fiftieth year, dug up an old photograph of its founders. There was a preacher, plump and smirky, and around him a handful of cheerful families. Ordinary, ordinary people: a doddering old banker, the proprietor of a ma-and-pa grocery, a straight-laced lady with a prim black Bible tucked under her arm, a bunch of kids making faces. But someone had scribbled a caption to the picture: "The Saints in Light," it read. "Thank God," shouts Colossians. "Thank God we have been qualified.... Saints in Light!"

Begin by admitting that we have been delivered from darkness. From the shadowy fears of childhood, from the grab and grasp of growing up, from adolescent memories we'd like to forget—we have been forgiven and set free. Goodness knows, we are not the best people in the world, but somehow we're able to love a little and, once in a while, usually on Sunday mornings, sense the mystery of God. A famous writer who was known for his unpleasantness was asked why, if he was Christian, he was not nicer. The writer answered, "My God, you don't know what I'd have been without my Lord and Savior Jesus Christ!" Well, most of us could echo the words. Somehow we have been delivered from darkness by the mercy of God. Now we are Christian people.

Has it occurred to you that maybe all along God has wanted a world full of Christian people—people who can love and live free for their neighbors, people like Jesus Christ. God made the world for Christ, that is what the Bible says. Like an artist who will make preliminary sketches before beginning a painting, so perhaps God drew the image of Christ as if to say, "That's the finished picture I have in mind!" Back before the world was, did God plan a universe for a people like Christ, who could trust God and in love be one with neighbors? Think it out; God made the world for Christ.

You know the story: Christ, the true image of God, was crucified. God painted an image of true humanity, and we deliberately slashed the picture. "Crucify him," we cried. Whatever God intended, we chose an image of our own desires. So when Christ came among us, we turned on him to destroy the image of God.

But here is the good news: Christ has been raised up. God's purpose has not changed. From the beginning, God wanted a people for communion. And, though we turned on God, God has turned toward us in mercy. Christ is risen and the whole creation is begun again, ruled by the image of God.

Now do you see who we are? We are members of Jesus Christ, much like other church people. But actually we are part of the world's new beginning. After the cross, we begin again, hearing Christ's word and sharing Christ's Spirit and growing into the image God intends. We are saints in light, sprung from darkness, now living as citizens of Christ's new humanity.

The language of Colossians is difficult. But we can declare the same soaring theology in our own everyday words.

GOSPEL: LUKE 23:35-43

Two traditions are included in the reading: the taunting of cross-bound Jesus (vv. 35-38), and the story of criminals crucified with Jesus (vv. 39-43). Both traditions include mention of Christ's kingship, appropriate for the observance of "Christ the King."

The account of the taunting is influenced by Psalm 22, a lament that includes mention of gambling for garments, pierced hands and feet, staring crowds, and mockery: "He committed his cause to the Lord; let him deliver him, let him rescue him . . ." (Ps. 22:8). No doubt the psalm much influenced the stories of Christ's crucifixion. Of course, the account of the taunting at the cross was also shaped as a reiteration of the temptation story (Luke 4:3, 9). Again, Jesus is tempted to prove his credentials—"If you really are the King of the Jews, save yourself. . . ." As the two traditions combine, we end up with three taunting temptations: by the leaders (v. 35), by the soldiers (v. 37), and, finally, by the first criminal (v. 39).

In vv. 35-38, titles are applied to Jesus. He is mocked as "God's Christ," "the Chosen One," and "the King of the Jews"—all messianic terms. But all the titles are spoken with heavy sarcasm: "He saved others. Let him save himself!" To hear the passage properly, we need a sound track of raucous laughter punctuating each sentence. Clearly, a naked, hung-up-to-die Jesus was a ludicrous figure compared to popular triumphant messianic expectations.

The story of the two criminals is found only in Luke. The account begins with a reiteration of mockery by the first criminal: "Are you not the Christ? Save yourself and us!" (Thus, Luke joins his sources.) The second criminal scolds him: "Don't you fear God?" He implies that, as they are condemned to death, they all will soon face divine judgment (v. 40). Then, he pronounces Christ's innocence, saying, in effect, though we are condemned justly and are only getting what we deserve, "This man has done nothing wrong" (v. 41).

The final cry of the second criminal is famous, "Jesus, remember me when you come into your kingdom." There is some debate over how the verse should be translated. Should it be "come in your kingdom," "come into your kingdom," or "come again as a king"? The RSV interprets the verse to read "come in your kingly power." Whatever the translation, the verse seems to be a pleading confession of faith.

Jesus answers, saying, "Amen. I say to you, today you will be with me in Paradise" (v. 43). He tosses the criminal a promise, as if to say, Today is the day of your salvation. We should not try to interpret the verse as a theological proof for immediate resurrection.

The word "paradise" is peculiar. The word derives from old Persian usage, where it referred to a spacious, enclosed park. The Septuagint uses the word of the Garden of Eden and also, in Ezek. 31:8, of "the garden of God," a place of fulfillment. In the intertestamental period, the word shows up in apocalyptic writings as a symbol of bliss in the new aeon. (In Christian Scriptures, it also appears in 2 Cor. 12:4 and Rev. 2:7.) So the word is a metaphor and should not be pressed into a precise definition of hereafter. After all, the key phrase in v. 43 is "you will be *with me.*" Ultimately, Christian hope is not a space for us, but communion with the Lord.

The problem for preaching is, how can we join the two traditions into a single sermon? If the taunting is based in part on triumphant messianic expectations—"King of the Jews"—then in the story of the criminals, we have a true definition of a messianic king. Christ is the king of a new age in which outcasts (criminals) are welcomed with mercy. He rules not by power but in love, a love that is radically self-giving.

A sermon might begin with scorn. (1) The man on the cross was not much of a king, even though the inscription read "King of the Jews." Most rulers are shrewd. They know how to promote themselves, how to dazzle a crowd. And they can use power to get things done. But Jesus was helpless. (2) No wonder people around the cross laughed. A naked, nailed-down Jesus was scarcely powerful. He was nothing more than a pretentious fool whose claims were utterly discredited by death. Hear the scorn that was heaped on him by a debunking world! (3) Yet, here we are in the twentieth century, proclaiming, "Jesus Christ is Lord." The one who was mocked, we lift up in praise. We set a crown above the cross in many of our churches. "King of kings," we call him. (4) Why? Because God has raised him up! He conquered death. He triumphed over massed evil. Condemned by the world, he is raised by God to be Lord of all. (5) We know because he has given us life; life defined by peace and love and mercy. Forgiven, free, and somehow made new—all because of Jesus, who died helpless on a cross. We believe that we are the Lord's and will be the Lord's people forever. "Today," we hear the voice of Christ saying, "Today you are mine forever."

Common Lectionary: John 12:9-19. This is a different passage for the celebration of "Christ the King," a passage from the Gospel of John. The structure of the passage is interesting: we have a "prologue" in vv. 9-11 and an "epilogue" in vv. 17-19. In between we have a story of Jesus' entry into Jerusalem, woven out of quotations from the Hebrew Scriptures (vv. 12-15). The story is followed by an "editorial note" in v. 16. Though Jesus is addressed as a king in the passage, John supplies a very different definition of kingship.

Notice the peculiar character of John's account of the "triumphal entry" compared to what we find in the Synoptic Gospels. In the Synoptics, the story is climactic, followed by Jesus' cleansing of the temple. In John, there have been prior visits to Jerusalem and thus, in this passage, no disruption of the temple. Instead, the crowd has been stirred by news of the raising of Lazarus, causing chief priests to plot death because "many of the Jews were going away and believing in Jesus" (v. 11).

The crowd, waving palms, comes out to greet Jesus. As there is little evidence for palm trees in Jerusalem, the reference is symbolic. Palms were a symbol of national liberation (see 1 Macc. 13:51; 2 Macc. 10:7). Jesus, then, is being greeted with "Hosannas" as a political leader. To underline the symbol, John adds the phrase "even the King of Israel" to the familiar quote from Psalm 118, "Blessed is he who comes in the name of the Lord!"

Then John redefines Jesus' messianic role. He offers an abridged quote from Zech. 9:9: "Fear not, daughter of Zion; behold, your king is coming, sitting on an ass's colt!" Significantly, John drops "triumphant and victorious is he" from the quotation. (He also deletes the word "humble," which also appears in Zechariah; humility is not the point here.) The important idea that John is promoting is to be found in the context of Zechariah's prophecy. The King will *not* come armed, riding in a war chariot, but will come as a peacegiver to the whole world (Zech. 9:10).

Verse 16 suddenly forces a reader (along with the disciples) to reflect on the story while recalling the cross-resurrection-ascension event that has created the new community of the Spirit in which we live. We realize that Jesus is not a power messiah who can ride a crest of rampant nationalism, but rather is one who gives new life (vv. 9, 17) and peace (v. 15) to the world. As the priests observe: "Look, the world has gone after him."

A sermon on the passage may well begin with the cries of the crowd; they thought they had found a liberator. Here comes a savior with clout who could make them great. If all the world were Israel (America), wouldn't that be salvation?

But, hold on, Jesus comes looking like a fool perched on a donkey. He is not waving from the turret of a tank in the midst of a ticker-tape parade. No, he comes weaponless on a farm animal. Of course, his entry into Jerusalem was nothing compared to the cross. He dies without force or fury, clinging to faith and forgiving his killers.

Maybe he is, after all, a different kind of liberator. Power in our world brandishes death and tramples the powerless. Jesus gives peace and, yes, life. We ought to know because we live in the church. We have no real clout in the world. But we study peace and, together, are beginning to live in a new way—by love.

We are called to follow the fool king on a donkey, and to hail his coming, so that someday the whole world will follow him into a life of peace. The story of the "triumphant entry" is full of irony. The crowd cheered Christ but for all the wrong reasons. Our job is to spread word of his coming so that a wider world may yet bow before him singing, "Blessed is he who comes in the name of the Lord!"